When I Go

When I Go

— Selected French Poems —

To Debby
It was great collaging and writing
with you — may this poetry keep
the inspiration going!

♡ Susanne
12-3-17

Rainer Maria Rilke

Translated with an Introduction by
Susanne Petermann

Foreword by
David H. Rosen

CASCADE *Books* · Eugene, Oregon

WHEN I GO
Selected French Poems

Cascade Books
An imprint of Wipf and Stock Publishers
199 W. 8th Ave., Suite 3
Eugene, OR 97401

www.wipfandstock.com

ISBN 13: 987-1-5326-0427-0 (paperback)
ISBN 13: 987-1-5326-0429-4 (hardcover)
ISBN 13: 987-1-5326-0428-7 (ebook)

Cataloging-in-Publication data:

Names: Rilke, Rainer Maria, 1875–1926, author | Petermann, Susanne, translator.

Title: When I go : selected French poems / Rainer Maria Rilke ; translated with an introduction by Susanne Petermann.

Description: Eugene, OR: Cascade Books, 2017 | Includes bibliographical data.

Identifiers: 987-1-5326-0427-0 (paperback) | 987-1-5326-0429-4 (hardcover) | 987-1-5326-0428-7 (ebook)

Subjects: LCSH: Poetry | Rilke, Rainer Maria, 1875–1926—Translations into English | French poetry—Translations into English.

Classification: PT2635 .I65 W57 2017 (print) | PT2635 (ebook).

Manufactured in the U.S.A.   08/17/17

Previous versions of some of these translations originally appeared in the following publications: *Agni, Arroyo, Cave Wall, Cerise, Dark Mountain, Epiphany*, the *Inflectionist Review, Inventory*, the *Jefferson Monthly, Jerseyworks*, the *Jung Journal of Culture and Psyche, Loaded Bicycle, Manzanita Quarterly, Passageways, Rhino, Rowboat, Solstice, To Topos Poetry International*, and *Transference*.

Contents

Foreword

What an honor to celebrate this collection of Rilke's French poems, *When I Go*. My association with Susanne came about through Rilke. As a Jungian analyst, I was reading *The Journal of Analytical Psychology* and there was an article on Rilke by Susanne. Her byline listed her name and said she was a "Professional Organizer." We were moving, so contacted her. She is a mover and shaker! Synchronicity was at work!

Susanne has become much larger than life. She became a translator, without training. And I became a poet with no training, as mine was in medicine. Later with William Carlos Williams as my mentor and my mother as a model (*Thin Mask* [New York: Crown Publications, 1939]).

Rilke is a favorite poet of mine. And I always loved his bow to the feminine. I had read Poulin's translation of his French poems, but found it lacking. So Susanne's translation is welcomed and needed. How grounding and liberating for Rilke to end up in the French part of Switzerland. The poet's last years were in a special place. These poems were planted and then blossomed and bore fruit in the Valais.

Over the years, I have read Susanne's refreshing translations. All of us await that day, when we go to that great beyond. It's clear from these end of life poems that he loved nature, as I do. What a joy to read "Roses," as my surname means just that. And the small pond in front of our small house in the woods has roses in two places, where you can sit, gaze and smell the roses.

—David H. Rosen

Acknowledgments

Deep gratitude to all who read these poems so generously. You comprise my writing tribe, and I dedicate this book to you.

To Sedonia Cahill and Beverly White, my dear departed teachers: you saw this book before I ever did. To Aaron Scott who offered a singularly poetic view, his brother Ramsey who was at the right place at the right time, and their parents Ginger and George who suffered through early versions but read them anyway. To the "Thursday Poets" Patricia Sempowich, Joyce Epstein, and Peggy Heiner for their unwavering support during our Monday meetings. To the Southern Oregon Women's Writers Group, Chorus and Gourmet Eating Society who have heard these poems more than anyone else: thanks for your gracious listening and wise, fierce feedback. To R. Ellis Dye, my college German professor, who I will always remember for lighting in me the eternal flame of the love of fine literature. To Priscilla Hunter and Lia Beeson, fellow translators who never let me lose hope for this project. To Rebecca Reilly and Joe Stroud for living and breathing your poetry and being willing to write blurbs. To French speakers Isabelle Alzado and Reneé Côté who helped me untangle Rilke's meanings, insofar as humanly possible. To Joanna Macy, Franz Wright, Robert Bly and Coleman Barks for their unsurpassed translations, and for writing back when I felt lost and confused. To Ray MacKenzie for being the first to read the whole manuscript and suggesting much-needed changes. To Susan Hagen, Story Woman, for helping me tell the story of these poems. To the late Al Poulin for being the first to collect all of Rilke's French poems into one book. To Anne Stine, whose wilderness work will change the world, with much love. To the Wild Hearts Circle who clucked and fussed and ceremonied every time I announced progress on this book. And to my most ardent supporter, life partner and companion on the writer's road, Holly Hertel: your love sustains me.

Introduction

"We could easily be made to believe that nothing happened, and yet we have changed, as a house that a guest has entered changes."[1]

Like many students of German literature, I sailed through college with a passing understanding of Rainer Maria Rilke's work. More than a dozen years of post-college adventures and foreign travels followed, until I finally landed in Los Angeles where I encountered these poems in a close, dusty bookstore, by sheer happenstance.

I didn't quite believe that Rilke had really written so much in French, so I bought the hefty volume, *The Complete French Poems*.[2] I read enough of it to learn that, yes, Rilke had written eight or nine series of poems and fragments (about 400 in all) in French shortly before he died. Before I could get very far, life intervened and the book lay half-forgotten among the others on my shelves, all of which tumbled to the floor a few months later, January 1994, during the Northridge earthquake. Luckily, I was living a few suburbs away from the epicenter, so, for me, results of the shaking were no worse than kitchen cupboards being emptied, a few dishes broken, and a living room floor littered with books. Exhausted from the shock and its aftermath, I sat down and opened Rilke's French poems quite at random.

I was looking for comfort in the musical words of the master I remembered from college; I wanted desperately to nourish myself with words, learn something by heart that would affirm and soften my inner state. Instead, I was dismayed to find that the translation conferred little of Rilke's melancholic charm and depth. Even more surprising was the discovery that

1. Rainer Maria Rilke, *Letters to a Young Poet,* trans. Stephen Mitchell (Boston: Shambala, 1993), 93–94.

2. Rainer Maria Rilke, *Complete French Poems of Rainer Maria Rilke*, trans. A. Poulin Jr. (Saint Paul: Graywolf, 1979).

I was holding in my hands the only existing English translation of these poems to date. And, it was a book that hadn't even been compiled until 1979, more than five decades after Rilke's death!

My curiosity was stirred. After all, I had just spent four uninterrupted years completely immersed in the French language while living in France and Casablanca. It was clear to me, when I compared the original to the translation, that these poems had not yet found the fullness of their expression in English. I set the book aside for further study, and over the next weeks and months, tentatively used a light pencil to change a word here and there.

Slowly the poems grew on me, and, with the encouragement of friends, I continued to re-translate them. It took years before I joined the American Literary Translators' Association and actually considered myself a translator. As a non-academic, I struggled to find my way through the translation process without the anchor or constraint of theory and background knowledge.

The process of taking the poems apart and putting them back together in my native English felt unfamiliar and difficult. But the poems kept pulling on me, and I craved guidance from the translators I loved to read. I decided to reach out. I wrote to Robert Bly and Coleman Barks asking them to direct me toward books, literary clubs, someone, *anyone* who could help. To my utter amazement, both men wrote back. A hand-typed letter on an old-fashioned half sheet of stationery bore a short message from Robert Bly, referring me to his excellent pamphlet, *The Eight Stages of Translation*,[3] which served as my only direct instruction on how to think about a poem while attempting to translate it.

From Coleman Barks came a postcard: "I'm retired now, but I certainly share your enthusiasm for Rilke. Good luck."

Later I wrote to Franz Wright, whose collection of translations, *The Unknown Rilke*[4]—far and away the best Rilke translations I have experienced—inspires me still. He had the humility to tell me that he'd been driven half-mad while translating Rilke, which, of course, had the effect on me of great encouragement. I will be forever grateful to these three poet-translators for their open-hearted responses to my efforts.

---

3. Robert Bly, *The Eight Stages of Translation* (Saint Paul: Ally, 1991).

4. Rainer Maria Rilke, *The Unknown Rilke: Expanded Edition*, trans. Franz Wright (Oberlin: Oberlin College Press, 1990).

This book includes five chapters: "Roses," "Windows," "Affectionate Tribute to France," "Valaisian Quatrains," and "Orchards." Rilke published these as separate books of poems, in some cases posthumously. There are a few exceptions to and repetitions in the way the poems are grouped together. I based my decisions on A. Poulin's book, with much gratitude for his pioneering efforts. The interested reader should refer to his introduction in *The Complete French Poems* for careful analysis and justification of the chapters and their chronology. I have included almost all the poems in each of the series, leaving out those poems I felt did not fit with the series due to the style or subject matter.

After two decades, I have not yet completed this project: there are almost two hundred French poems I have not included in this book. I am a bit chagrined about the amount of time it has taken me. But Rilke himself justifies the slowness of the creative process, exhorting the artist to avoid guilt and pressure, to embrace unencumbered time, even fallow periods and apparent indolence to let the work rest and mature. All of these poems have become long-term guests in my house, and even when I am not interacting with them directly, they are acting on me.

Rilke

> Rilke is an explosive experience . . . and it is as music that Rilke
> is best approached; let the reader give himself to the rhythm, the
> melody, and the exaltation of the poems; the understanding will
> follow."[5]

So much is known about Rilke's fifty-one-year sojourn on this earth. His *Collected Works* fill six dense volumes that don't even include his letters, which are estimated to number an astonishing 11,000 by translator Ulrich Baer. Numerous biographers have filled thousands of pages with every detail of his life. Countless translations (of his German works) each include biographies of various lengths.

It would take years for even the most ardent researcher to slog through the many interpretive critical articles. What was important to me was to stay with my private experience as I read through the French poems, supplementing my knowledge from time to time with biographical writings.

5. Rainer Maria Rilke, *Fifty Selected Poems: Rainer Maria Rilke*, trans. C. F. MacIntyre (Berkeley: University of California, 1941), 16.

This man was a twentieth century literary force comparable to a fire that creates its own weather system. In this case, his literary output unleashed a firestorm of opinions from gushing admiration to contempt, based on stories about him that were sometimes just myths.

I will focus here on merely outlining the aspects of Rilke's trajectory that pointed to his last years in Switzerland where he produced most of the French poems. He was born in December, 1875, in Prague. The name given him, René Karl Wilhelm Johann Josef Maria Rilke, betrays his Catholic heritage and echoes his family's origin stretching from Alsace to Moravia.

Indeed, there was never a feeling in this family that Prague was home. Socially, his mother fancied herself of royal blood and was consumed with resentment about her husband's lack of status and career ambition. She did, however, give little René the gift of teaching him French even before he went to school.

Geographically and culturally, the poet always disparaged Prague as a backwater. The young Rilke suffered the push-pull of conflict between his mother's extreme sentimentalism and religiosity, and his father's hopes that he be groomed for the ranks of officialdom. He was sent away to military school. By age eighteen, he had rebelled and begun to seek artistic stimulation by traveling and living in far-flung places from Moscow to Pisa.

To say that Rilke was compelled to write is to understate his drive. He prioritized his writing over everything else, so that, even when he married and had a daughter, he couldn't shake the feeling of being separated from his work. He felt trapped and isolated within the confines of the young family and left their home in northern Germany, never to return.

Franz Wright says that Rilke transcends his reputation as either a "chaste and solitary high priest of art" or as a "kept man who flitted back and forth between the estates of adoring, wealthy women."[6] His dedication was unwavering and he was adored and supported by readers from the time he began publishing in his early twenties. True, he was often devastatingly lonely and, for most of his life, homeless. But he cultivated connection with anyone who would engage him, from famous contemporary poets to lowly housemaids, in philosophical, artistic and spiritual discussion. His many letters prove my point, as do these heartfelt poems.

He moved to Paris, first in 1902, then again in 1905, where he worked as informal secretary for the sculptor, Auguste Rodin. The position did not

6. Rainer Maria Rilke, *The Unknown Rilke: Expanded Edition*, trans. Franz Wright (Oberlin: Oberlin College Press, 1990), 9, 10.

suit him. The two men admired each other, but fought and disagreed and suffered miscommunications.

However, it was during these years that Rilke began, with Rodin's prompting, to serve his poetry by observing the world. He thought about this as an exercise of "saying" the world of things, scrupulously avoiding personal reaction, Victorian-style symbolism, and anthropomorphism. Instead, he entered the world of the thing while simultaneously retaining his own humanity and giving the "thing" its own existence.

This is a simple idea which I find very hard to explain. I rely on the metaphor of the mirror to understand it: the world is a mirror, and the poet took it upon himself to look into it honestly. The poems of this period, published in a volume called *New Poems,* were called *Dinggedichte*, "thing-poems." With this publication, he made his mark on the history of literature, firmly breaking with the Romantics he had grown up reading.

Until late 1915, in spite of chronic melancholy, he had already completed at least three of his most famous cycle of poems, the *Duino Elegies.* But the darkness and humiliation of WWI plunged him into deep emotional and creative despair. He stopped work on the *Elegies,* renounced German culture and language, which angered many of his supporters, and moved to French-speaking Switzerland, in the Canton of Valais.

There, a benefactor set him up at Muzot, a small stone house. It was ancient, drafty, and isolated. But it was here that his long and tortured silence finally broke open in an incredible ten-day outburst that resulted in the completion of the *Duino Elegies* and a whole new series of poems, the *Sonnets to Orpheus.*

It was February 1922. He knew immediately after completing these two cycles that his position on the literary map was forever secured. In the four years that remained of his life, he wrote 325 poems and about 75 fragments and dedications in French.

Why French?

> How can it be explained that a mature poet, who at that time of his life had an unexcelled power over his native language, would give up his own perfected instrument to try another?[7]

7. Liselotte Dieckmann, "Rainer Maria Rilke's French Poems," *Modern Language Quarterly* 12 (1951) 321.

Perhaps his personal breakthrough and widespread acclaim caused something inside Rilke's being to relax, because it was then that he began to write seriously in French. The switch was quite abrupt, like a visual artist leaving behind the oil paints to take up watercolors. Rilke grew more and more outspoken in his enthusiasm for the French language, especially following encouragement by French poets André Gide and Paul Valéry. Biographer Donald Prater writes that "he compared French with 'a beautiful vine ripened over the centuries' and cultivated according to well-defined laws: a language with a clarity and sureness which his own was far from having achieved."[8]

Translator Willis Barnstone says that, once translated, a poem becomes an orphan stripped of its history. If that's true, the poems in this book are doubly orphaned because Rilke wrote in his second language while ignoring the heavy historical context of centuries of French literary tradition.

There are at least two instances where Rilke spoke directly about why he switched to French late in his life. Following the political turmoil of WWI, he wrote: "How *very much* I hate this people [the Germans] . . . Nobody will ever be able to claim that I write in *their* language!"[9]

Second, he considered a handful of French words uniquely beautiful by their untranslatable nature, including "orchard," and "palm." In the title poem of his series, "Orchards" *[Vergers],* he begins this way:

> Perhaps, dear borrowed language,
> I've been emboldened to use you because
> of the rustic word whose unique domain
> has taunted me forever: *Verger.*

In addition, we can imagine the healing effect on Rilke of the rolling hills, vineyards and hospitality of the Valais. He'd completed his greatest works at Muzot, his first real home, a place of refuge where he was to live out his remaining years in spite of a life-long habit of restlessness.

This French-speaking region of Switzerland seemed refreshingly untouched by the war. He was so enamored of the place that he even changed his citizenship. He planted roses, he walked the lanes through the vineyards, he watched and wrote about the wind and sky.

---

8. Donald Prater, *A Ringing Glass* (New York: Oxford University Press, 1986), 363.

9. Rainer Maria Rilke, *Letters on Life*, trans. Ulrich Baer (New York: Random House, 2005), xix.

I suspect there may be one more partial answer to the question, "Why French?": Rilke's relationship to a woman named Elisabeth Dorothée Kossowska, known by the nicknames Baladine, Merline, or Mouky. Like Rilke, she had a Germanic background and for political and philosophical reasons that closely aligned with Rilke's, came to reject that culture. Their passionate exchange of letters in French (published in Zürich in 1954) filled the intervals between their meetings and would last until the end of his life.

Some have claimed that French, for Rilke, was a mere game or language exercise, but I don't believe it, given the quality of the poems. Rilke's French was good. He rarely made errors, and like any poet or literary figure, puts his mark on the language and expands it, adds to it his own flavor. Nor does his French sound or feel like German, though some critics disagree. He was not unduly influenced by any particular French author, in spite of his close relationship with Paul Valéry whose poems he translated at the time he was producing his French poems. He was praised by Valéry, André Gide, and Jean Cocteau. Liselotte Dieckmann writes: "A bold originality characterizes Rilke's poems; he shows a mastery of the adopted language which he uses freely as an instrument of genuine poetic expression."[10]

Dieckmann also says this: "The poet was forced, by the nature of his relationship to the new language, to write simple poetry; and at the same time, the trend towards simplicity appears as the natural relief after the overwhelming task which the *Elegies* had put before him. A feeling of happy relaxation goes through the French poems; . . . The French language, besides being a new instrument for the poet, has the advantage over the German language of offering a simplicity of style as well as of verse form without becoming trite or overly plain."[11]

This corresponds with what I persistently felt as I translated the French poems. I sensed no literary baggage; there was a light feeling to them, even when the subject was melancholy, even gloomy.

Lastly, we should perhaps be asking whether the question "Why French?" really matters. Americans, especially writers and linguists, who have spent time in Europe, know that competency in other languages is not unusual there.

During an exchange of letters between Rilke and Russian poet Marina Tsvetaeva, she writes: "Dear Rainer, Goethe says somewhere that one cannot achieve anything of significance in a foreign language—and that has

10. Dieckmann, "Rainer Maria Rilke's French Poems," 321.
11. Ibid., 328.

always rung false to me . . . Writing poetry is in itself translating from the mother tongue into another, whether French or German should make no difference . . ."[12]

Translation Priorities

Translation is gratitude to language.[13]

The difficulty of translating Rilke will cause the heart of any Rilke translator—and there are many, though not of the French poems—to lurch with recognition, affection and dread. To give a specific example, "The Doe" [*La Biche*], begins, in French:

> Ô la biche: quel bel intérieur
> d'anciennes forêts dans tes yeux abonde;
> combien de confiance ronde
> mêlée à combien de peur.

Literally: "Oh, the doe: what a beautiful interior / of ancient forests in your eyes abounds; / how much round confidence / mixed with how much fear." To begin with, there is the Ô and the *quel,* followed by two occurrences of *combien,* all of which lend a tone of breathless drama. I acknowledge the Romantic style of Rilke's poetic heritage, but there are other ways to convey urgency in this poem. Personally, I am far more interested in the fact that this poet sees a deer and offers us a unique perspective on the mystery inherent in its being.

Gary Miranda, a translator I admire, gave us a marvelous new version of Rilke's *Duino Elegies.* In his afterword, he says this, on the pesky subject of Ô: ". . . a modern American reader has far less tolerance for 'O' than a European reader of Rilke's day, and one has to assume that Rilke would have been sensitive to that fact had he been writing for a modern American audience. So, if you're aiming to approximate the original experience for a modern audience, you're going to have to jettison some of those Os. This is

---

12. Art Beck, "Essay: How Not to Review a Translation," *Your Impossible Voice,* http://www.yourimpossiblevoice.com/essay-not-review-translation.

13. Nancy Naomi Carlson, as overheard at the 39th annual conference of the American Literary Translators' Association, 2016.

just one reason that it's always seemed silly to me to talk about a definitive translation. Definitive for whom?"[14]

In addition to the issue of overly heightened drama, I spent a long time contemplating the deceptively simple word choices in this poem. The most obvious translations did not offer the best poetry. Case in point: the French word *intérieur*, "interior" or "inside": the more I studied this poem, the more I felt that this word stuck out and gave the line a scientific tone that clashed with the simplicity and darkness of a Grimm's fairy-tale forest, glimpsed by the poet in the black eyes of the doe.

I wrote version after version, and finally tried not using the word "interior" at all while retaining the concept. This required rearranging the lines a bit, and including the idea of "inside" with the quieter preposition "in," and by adding the adjective "deep." As for the drama of the original, my hope is that I have transferred that feeling to the third and fourth lines of the verse, using the short and emphatic "shot through" and "utter fear."

> Doe, the deep, ancient beauty
> of forests flows in your eyes,
> circles of trust shot through
> with utter fear.

My priority in translation is that the poems must be poems in English. I conformed almost without exception to Rilke's line and stanza breaks, and I gave a good amount of attention to rhythm. For Rilke, rhyme and meter represented pleasurable constraints.

But translating his exact rhymes was never my goal; in my view this tended to distort these short verses beyond poetic tolerance. I am satisfied with (the sometimes accidental) resonances such as those between "doe" and "deep," and "forests" and "flows."

In general, I have emphasized flow and content, striking what I perceived to be a balance between the numerous difficulties of translation. I did not want to adhere so strictly to accuracy that I would end up performing, so to speak, an operation that killed the patient.

My goal was to communicate musicality through occasional and oblique rhymes, loose internal rhymes, repeating vowel sounds, and rhythmic patterns. These poems are a vast and intricate house, and rather than

---

14. Rainer Maria Rilke, *Duino Elegies*, trans. Gary Miranda (Portland, OR: Tavern, 2013), 66–67.

guide you on a tour of all its nooks and crannies, I hope I have merely held open its door, offering a fresh journey of discovery aided by language.

The Journey

Now you must go out into your heart / as onto a vast plain.[15]

Rilke was absolutely opposed to any form of analysis, psychological or otherwise. He rejected the budding field that Sigmund Freud was advertising and some of his friends promoting. Yet, he was ahead of his time, because, through pure intuition, he found a natural affinity between psychology and spirituality that has become mainstream in our modern culture.

Many of his writings sound as though they could have come from a book of Buddhist or Taoist teachings. Ulrich Baer tells the story that in 1908, Rilke's wife (with whom he stayed friendly) sent him *Speeches by Gotama Buddha*. Rilke closed it almost as soon as he had opened it, not because he disliked the ideas he found in the book, but, according to Baer, because he experienced a "shudder of recognition," intuiting that the ideas were too close to his own.

So, Rilke followed the deep river of his thought without asking why or how. In much the same way, I translated his poetry without knowing how to translate.

My journey through these poems has imparted not only lessons in translation, but lessons in life. Getting behind Rilke's messages and meanings required me to read the poems deeply, many times over. I would take each one in turn, copy it out by hand, and go for a long walk to memorize it and get the rhythms in my body.

During the most intense periods of translation, I felt I was not translating at all, but writing poems with the guidance of a wise person who'd given me some ideas about what I should say. This process also had the effect of planting seeds from which my own, original poetry grew.

I can't help being continually amazed at how skillfully Rilke held the extremes of spirituality and physicality in one hand. His eyes took in the outer world, and whether it was panther, rose or embroidered shawl, those observations enriched his inner life. In his worldview, nature becomes its

15. Rainer Maria Rilke, *Rilke's Book of Hours*, trans. Anita Barrows and Joanna Macy (New York: Penguin, 2005), 133.

own powerful, multi-faceted being that does not exist for our benefit, but has the effect, if we allow the mirror to work on our psyche, of deepening and nourishing us.

The subjects Rilke treats in these poems are alive with profound history, intricate rhythms, loves and preferences, none of which are completely known either by the poet or by us. There is freedom in this, and the possibility of union between humanity and something higher.

The integration of the spiritual and physical realms has always held intense interest for me, and there is no better context in which to experience this coming together than in wild nature.

Each August, I help facilitate a two-week wilderness experience for a group of women who are questing for a new life. We mark turning points such as divorce, the departure of children to college, the end of child-bearing years, or even, simply, a birthday. Though each woman's goal is personal, life in the wilderness requires community and careful attention to the physical plane. Our concerns revolve around eating, sleeping, staying warm; fuel, water, safety. Solitude is an important component of this rite of passage, for in the face of these situations we are all fundamentally alone.

Rilke, it is well known, cherished his solitude and wrestled with his inner demons through the process of contemplating the simple, every-day objects of his life—the painting above the mantle or the water jug and drinking glass. He did not deny the body, as the Romantics had done.

Ulrich Baer says: "Rilke finds evidence of a connectedness to larger, cosmic patterns within our physical, bodily existence. How we breathe, eat, sleep, digest, and love; how we suffer physically or experience pleasure."[16]

It turns out the two poles of concern, physical and spiritual, do not work against each other. The mundane becomes sacred and the sacred mundane. That which we see, sees us. Watching an ant can change a life. Fetching a drink of water can quench the soul. The act of writing a poem confirms the poet's as well as the subject's existence in equal measure, as it confirms creation throughout all time.

I feel undying gratitude to Rilke, my teacher from the beyond. His voice has scarcely diminished in volume since his death ninety years ago this month. Here it is, with us again, the same and brand new, showing

---

16. Rainer Maria Rilke, *Letters on Life,* trans. Ulrich Baer (New York: Random House, 2005), xxiii.

us the way to live with our longing and to see, albeit slowly, into our true selves.

S.P.
Medford, Oregon
December 2016

I

Roses

Still—in a way—nobody sees a flower—really—it is so small—
we haven't time—and to see takes time, like to have a friend takes time.[1]

O ne of the myths that circle around Rilke concerns the cause of his
death. In cutting roses from his garden at Muzot for his newest love
interest, he was pricked by a thorn, which turned into a nasty infection.

Biographer Ralph Freedman writes: "For ten days both hands were
unusable, after which he caught an intestinal flu with a high fever. It is un-
likely that the thorn itself caused Rilke's death, as is romantically assumed,
but it may well have triggered attacks from which, in the end, he did not
recover."[2]

Rilke harbored distrust of doctors and hospitals, and suffered unnec-
essarily before a rare form of leukemia took his life in December 1926. He
is buried in the village church at Raron, in Valais.

Whatever part roses may have played in Rilke's demise, it is especially
poignant that, in this series of twenty-seven poems, Rilke expresses a pas-
sion to live the creative life. At the time of their writing, death was not yet
sitting on his shoulder. Death remains a theme, an abstraction.

The *Roses* orbit around beauty and life-force like perfumed pet-
als around a stamen, making me a bit dizzy with ecstasy and optimism

1. Georgia O'Keeffe, from the Exhibit Catalogue of the show "An American Place,"
1939.

2. Ralph Freedman, *Life of a Poet* (Evanston, IL: Northwestern University Press,
1996), 546.

whenever I read them. I feel like the "Round Rose": "Doesn't it make you dizzy... /to spin and spin upon your stem...?"

The images are often overtly erotic, speaking fearlessly of "inner caresses," "the ultimate mouth," "Narcissus' fulfillment," "the bud that is you," the flower that "between two lovers expires." Like arms encircling the beloved, Rilke's roses bring together physical desire and spiritual longing—two opposing realms which, in his day, were kept safely apart. He usurps the religious language of praise usually reserved for deity: each rose is a "whole and perfect thing," the "essence supreme of this fleeting existence," "worthy of being a reliquary," comparable to a "naked saint." The rose could also be a prickly lover: "Against whom have you adopted these thorns?"

In praising roses, the poet also praises humanity; they are "of the earth, like us, after all." Just as we write poems and paint paintings, the rose "builds [herself] a space" made of perfumed abundance. Through no effort, both roses and humans are "inward makers of more of [ourselves]."

That said, Rilke is never just sweetness and light. The rose points the way toward death, shows us that the door to all knowing opens in the paradox of "the ineffable connection between nothingness and existence." Indeed, the rose is the centerpiece of Rilke's famous epitaph: "Rose, oh pure contradiction / joy to be nobody's sleep / beneath so many lids."

Your Freshness

If your freshness sometimes stuns us,
glad rose,
it's that deep within,
petal on petal, you are resting.

Fully awake while their center sleeps,
countless tender feelings
of the quiet heart touch
and converge in the ultimate mouth.

I

Si ta fraîcheur parfois nous étonne tant,
heureuse rose,
c'est qu'en toi-même, en dedans,
pétale contre pétale, tu te reposes.

Ensemble tout éveillé, dont le milieu
dort, pendant qu'innombrables, se touchent
les tendresses de ce cœur silencieux
qui aboutissent à l'extrême bouche.

Half-Open Book

I see you, rose, half-open book,
pages full
of detailed joy
no one will ever read. Book of magic,

opened by wind and readable
even with closed eyes . . .
bewildered butterflies leave you,
having had the same ideas.

II

Je te vois, rose, livre entrebâillé,
qui contient tant de pages
de bonheur détaillé
qu'on ne lira jamais. Livre-mage,

qui s'ouvre au vent et qui peut être lu
les yeux fermés . . . ,
dont les papillons sortent confus
d'avoir eu les mêmes idées.

Whole and Perfect Thing

O rose, you whole and perfect thing,
infinitely self-contained
and infinitely expanding, O head
so tender, the body disappears,

you have no equal, essence supreme
of this floating existence.
Around this space of love we can barely cross,
your perfume makes a full circle.

III

Rose, toi, ô chose par excellence complète
qui se contient infiniment
et qui infiniment se répand, ô tête
d'un corps par trop de douceur absent,

rien ne te vaut, ô toi, suprême essence
de ce flottant séjour;
de cet espace d'amour où à peine l'on avance
ton parfum fait le tour.

The Challenge

We're the ones who dared you
to refill your calyx.
Charmed, your abundance
accepted the challenge.

Your wealth was such that you became
a hundred selves in a single flower;
that's the way of the lover . . .
you never had any other.

IV

C'est pourtant nous qui t'avons proposé
de remplir ton calice.
Enchantée de cet artifice,
ton abondance l'avait osé.

Tu étais assez riche, pour devenir cent fois toi-même
en une seule fleur;
c'est l'état de celui qui aime . . .
Mais tu n'as pas pensé ailleurs.

Ecstasy

Ecstasy on ecstasy,
tenderness on tenderness . . .
we could say that your interior
never stops caressing itself

with inner caresses.
You light your own reflection.
Thus you've invented
Narcissus' fulfillment.

V

Abandon entouré d'abandon,
tendresse touchant aux tendresses . . . .
C'est ton intérieur qui sans cesse
se caresse, dirait-on;

se caresse en soi-même,
par son propre reflet éclairé.
Ainsi tu inventes le thème
du Narcisse exaucé.

One Rose

One rose is every rose
and here: the irreplaceable one,
perfect, a supple word
encased in a context of things.

Without her, how could we ever speak
of bygone hopes,
of the tender intervals between
farewells that never end.

VI

Une rose seule, c'est toutes les roses
et celle-ci: l'irremplaçable,
le parfait, le souple vocable
encadré par le texte des choses.

Comment jamais dire sans elle
ce que furent nos espérances,
et les tendres intermittences
dans la partance continuelle.

Holding You

Holding you against my eyelid,
cool, clear rose,
like a thousand eyelids
superimposed

on my warm one,
your thousand sleeps against the illusion
that I prowl
a fragrant labyrinth.

VII

T'appuyant, fraîche claire
rose, contre mon oeil fermé—,
on dirait mille paupières
superposées

contre la mienne chaude.
Mille sommeils contre ma feinte
sous laquelle je rôde
dans l'odorant labyrinthe.

Drunk on Your Dream

Flower drunk on your dream,
filled with many selves,
moist as a mourner,
leaning on the dawn.

With hesitant desire
your gentle powers sleep,
forming all the tenderness
between breasts and cheeks.

VIII

De ton rêve trop plein,
fleur en dedans nombreuse,
mouillée comme une pleureuse,
tu te penches sur le matin.

Tes douces forces qui dorment,
dans un désir incertain,
développent ces tendres formes
entre joues et seins.

Rose, All Passion

Rose, all passion, yet pure,
worthy of being the reliquary
of St. Rose, you exude
the troubling perfume of naked saint.

Rose beyond temptation, disconcertingly
peaceful inside; ultimate lover
so far from Eve and her first warning—
rose holding permanent claim to the fall.

IX

Rose, toute ardente et pourtant claire,
que l'on devrait nommer reliquaire
de Sainte-Rose . . . rose qui distribue
cette troublante odeur de sainte nue.

Rose plus jamais tentée, déconcertante
de son interne paix; ultime amante,
si loin d'Ève, de sa première alerte—,
rose qui infiniment possède la perte.

Friend

Friend in lonely hours
when everything rejects the jaded heart,
she proves her consoling presence
with many airy caresses.

If we refuse to live, if we deny
what has been and what could be,
we've forgotten this persistent friend,
working her magic at our side.

X

Amie des heures où aucun être ne reste,
où tout se refuse au cœur amer;
consolatrice dont la présence atteste
tant de caresses qui flottent dans l'air.

Si l'on renonce à vivre, si l'on renie
ce qui était et ce qui peut arriver,
pense-t-on jamais assez à l'insistante amie
qui à côté de nous fait son oeuvre de fée.

My Being

My being so dwells on you
perfect rose,
that I confuse my feeling for you
with my festive heart.

I inhale you, rose,
like life itself,
and I feel I'm the perfect friend
to such a friend.

XI

J'ai une telle conscience de ton
être, rose complète,
que mon consentement te confond
avec mon cœur en fête.

Je te respire comme si tu étais,
rose, toute la vie,
et je me sens l'ami parfait
d'une telle amie.

Against Whom

Rose, against whom
have you adopted
these thorns?
Has the extreme
refinement of your joy
forced you into
arms?

And from whom does this excessive
weaponry protect you?
How many enemies
have I chased away from you
who had no fear at all?
Yet from summer to fall
you lash out at the care
we give you.

XII

Contre qui, rose,
avez-vous adopté
ces épines?
Votre joie trop fine
vous a-t-elle forcée
de devenir cette chose
armée?

Mais de qui vous protège
cette arme exagérée?
Combien d'ennemis vous ai-je

enlevés
qui ne la craignaient point.
Au contraire, d'été en automne,
vous blessez les soins
qu'on vous donne.

Who Are You?

Rose, are you our chaperone
in the throes of emotional transport?
Or would you rather be a souvenir
of a pleasant moment?

Often I see you, dry and content,
—each petal a shroud—
in a fragrant box with a lock of hair,
or in a favorite book reread alone.

XIII

Préfères-tu, rose, être l'ardente compagne
de nos transports présents?
Est-ce souvenir qui davantage te gagne
lorsqu'un bonheur se reprend?

Tant de fois je t'ai vue, heureuse et sèche,
—chaque pétale un linceul—
dans un coffret odorant, à côté d'une mèche,
ou dans un livre aimé qu'on relira seul.

Summer

Summer: to sojourn
alongside the roses,
inhaling the aura
of their blossoming souls,

hearing the last word
of each one that dies,
and surviving that sister
in others to come.

XIV

Été: être pour quelques jours
le contemporain des roses;
respirer ce qui flotte autour
de leurs âmes écloses.

Faire de chacune qui se meurt
une confidente,
et survivre à cette sœur
en d'autres roses absentes.

Abundant Flower

You build yourself a space,
O abundant flower;
you see yourself in a mirror
of scent.

Like petals, perfume surrounds
your multiple calyx.
I hold you back, you expand,
you astonishing actress.

XV

Seule, ô abondante fleur,
tu crées ton propre espace;
tu te mires dans une glace
d'odeur.

Ton parfum entoure comme d'autres pétales
ton innombrable calice.
Je te retiens, tu t'étales,
prodigieuse actrice.

Ineffable

Let's not talk about you. You're ineffable
by nature.
You transform the table
other flowers merely adorn.

We place you in a simple vase
and everything changes:
the very same words
now sung by an angel.

XVI

Ne parlons pas de toi. Tu es ineffable
selon ta nature.
D'autres fleurs ornent la table
que tu transfigures.

On te met dans un simple vase—,
voici que tout change:
c'est peut-être la même phrase,
mais chantée par un ange.

You're the One

You're the one, the inward maker
of more of yourself, your ultimate essence.
The uneasiness emerging from you
is your dance.

Each petal consents
and takes a few steps
in the wind, fragrant,
invisible.

O music to the eyes,
amidst all these petals
you become
intangible.

XVII

C'est toi qui prépares en toi
plus que toi, ton ultime essence.
Ce qui sort de toi, ce troublant émoi,
c'est ta danse.

Chaque pétale consent
et fait dans le vent
quelques pas odorants
invisibles.

Ô musique des yeux,
toute entourée d'eux,
tu deviens au milieu
intangible.

We Know Nothing

You share all our emotions,
but we know nothing of your life.
We'd have to be a hundred butterflies
to read each of your pages.

The dictionaries among you
are gathered by those
who'd prefer to bind all these pages together.
As for me, I prefer epistolary roses.

XVIII

Tout ce qui nous émeut, tu le partages.
Mais ce qui t'arrive, nous l'ignorons.
Il faudrait être cent papillons
pour lire toutes tes pages.

Il y en a d'entre vous qui sont comme des dictionnaires;
ceux qui les cueillent
ont envie de faire relier toutes ces feuilles.
Moi, j'aime les roses épistolaires.

Example

Are you volunteering to be our example?
Can we fulfill ourselves like roses do,
multiplying spiritual matter
just by being?

It seems there's no work
to being a rose.
God makes the house
by looking out the window.

XIX

Est-ce en exemple que tu te proposes?
Peut-on se remplir comme les roses,
en multipliant sa subtile matière
qu'on avait faite pour ne rien faire?

Car ce n'est pas travailler que d'être
une rose, dirait-on.
Dieu, en regardant par la fenêtre,
fait la maison.

What Is the Source?

Tell me, rose, what is the source
of your blossoming,
the deep, slow essence that imposes
so many airy delights
on this space of prose?

The same air often claims
to be jabbed by this or that,
or makes a show of bitterness
with a pout.
But, exposed to your flesh,
Rose, it struts around.

XX

Dis-moi, rose, d'où vient
qu'en toi-même enclose,
ta lente essence impose
à cet espace en prose
tous ces transports aériens?

Combien de fois cet air
prétend que les choses le trouent,
ou, avec une moue,
il se montre amer.
Tandis qu'autour de ta chair,
Rose, il fait la roue.

Round Rose

Doesn't it make you dizzy, round rose,
to spin and spin upon your stem
until you are finished?
Overwhelmed by your momentum,

you don't know the bud that is you.
It's a world that whirls around,
its calm center daring
the round rose its round repose.

XXI

Cela ne te donne-t-il pas le vertige
de tourner autour de toi sur ta tige
pour te terminer, rose ronde?
Mais quand ton propre élan t'inonde,

tu t'ignores dans ton bouton.
C'est un monde qui tourne en rond
pour que son calme centre ose
le rond repos de la ronde rose.

The Earth of the Dead

Rose, again you rise
from the earth of the dead,
you who bring
convincing joy

to the day of gold.
And they whose concave skulls
never suspected a thing,
do they approve?

XXII

Vous encore, vous sortez
de la terre des morts,
rose, vous qui portez
vers un jour tout en or

ce bonheur convaincu.
L'autorisent-ils, eux
dont le crâne creux
n'en a jamais tant su?

Late-Blooming Rose

Late-blooming rose whom the bitter nights slow
with their sidereal light,
can you guess at the full and easy pleasure
of your summer sisters?

For days and days I watched you hesitate
as your sheath grew too tight.
Rose, you turn backward at birth to borrow
the slow pace of death.

Does the chaos of your multiplicity
show you the ineffable connection
between nothingness and existence
that we will never know?

XXIII

Rose, venue très tard, que les nuits amères arrêtent
par leur trop sidérale clarté,
rose, devines-tu les faciles délices complètes
de tes sœurs d'été ?

Pendant des jours et des jours je te vois qui hésites
dans ta gaine serrée trop fort.
Rose qui en naissant, à rebours imites
les lenteurs de la mort.

Ton innombrable état te fait-il connaître
dans un mélange où tout se confond,
cet ineffable accord du néant et de l'être
que nous ignorons?

26

Rose of the Earth

Rose of the earth, like us, after all,
flower of all flowers,
do you feel, inwardly, petal on petal,
our palpable joy?

Do the soft sensations that fill you, O rose,
add up to an understanding
of all we've dared and all that we dare,
and this hesitant pleasure?

XXIV

Rose, terrestre pourtant, à nous autres égale,
fleur de toutes nos fleurs,
est-ce que tu sens en toi, pétale contre pétale,
nos palpables bonheurs.

Ces attouchements doux qui te remplissent, ô rose,
est-ce que leur somme comprend
tout ce qu'on avait osé, tout ce que l'on ose
et le plaisir hésitant?

Dear to Our Traditions

Rose, dear to our traditions,
dedicated to our fondest memories,
becoming imaginary and so able
to weave into our dreams—

silent rose, better than song
when infusing the air,
queen of rose windows
that between two lovers expires.

XXV

Rose, à nos habitudes si chère,
à nos plus chers souvenirs dédiée,
devenue presque imaginaire
pour être tant à nos rêves liées—,

Rose qui, silencieuse, surpasse
en se mêlant à l'air, les chants,
qui triomphe dans la rosace
et qui meurt entre deux amants.

The Opening Rose

Unendingly secure
despite many dangers,
without ever changing
her usual way,
the opening rose is a prelude
to her innumerable days.

Who knows how many she lives?
One of her days, surely,
is all of earth and all
the infinity of here.

XXVI

Infiniment rassurée
malgré tant de dangers
sans jamais rien changer
à ses habitudes,
la rose qui s'ouvre, prélude
à son innombrable durée.

Sait-on combien elle vit?
Un de ses jours, sans doute,
c'est toute la terre, toute
l'infinité d'ici.

Here You Are

Dear exquisite rose, did you have
to be left outside?
What is a rose doing here,
where fate exhausts us?

There's no going back. Here you are
desperately sharing our lives,
this life and these times
where you don't belong.

XXVII

Rose, eut-il fallu te laisser dehors,
chère exquise?
Que fait une rose là où le sort
sur nous s'épuise?

Point de retour. Te voici
qui partages
avec nous, éperdue, cette vie, cette vie
qui n'est pas de ton âge.

2

Windows

Isn't it time our loving freed us from the one we love and we,
trembling, endured . . . because to stay is to be nowhere.[3]

This series was inspired by Rilke's French-speaking lover Baladine. It begins romantically enough with a vision of a woman spotted through a high window on a balcony, unreachable, a graceful long-haired figure who reminds us of a painful loss that still feels fresh.

Our triggered memory, plus the actual image of the woman seen through the window, superimposed upon what is reflected in the glass—the street, gardens, water—all of these add up to layers that are not quite clearly seen but acutely felt.

The gift of the window, it turns out, is not only our view of days and nights and seasons, but the stark fact of its limiting geometry, its "simple shape [circumscribing] effortlessly this enormous life." Here is a rectangle within whose confines our longing finds meaning, a "center of love" making us feel safe and balanced.

But there is a price to pay for this sheltered feeling. First, the burden of choice: should we stay within this "geometry," or go beyond it? "Who would [we] be waiting for?" We wake to the frightening, tantalizing reality of the "road that beckons," a "glimpse of freedom." Suddenly, our dreams may come true; the nightmare of death seems possible. The infinite world

3. Donald Prater, *A Ringing Glass* (New York: Oxford University Press, 1986), 205.

on the far side of the window could make us "drink [our] whole abyss," "turn [us] to wind, pour [us] in the river."

Rilke praises the window for the paradox that has scared us half to death. He turns it into a new constellation, as strange as a new number, and sends it into the heavens for us to worship. Henceforth, the window serves as an ironic gift: limitless possibility within a limited framework, like poetry contained within rhyme and meter.

All It Takes

All it takes is a woman
pausing slightly
on a balcony or in a window frame,
to be the one we've lost
the moment she appears.

And if she lifts her arms
to tie up her hair,
tender vase, how suddenly
our grief sharpens
and our sorrow flares!

I

Il suffit que, sur un balcon
ou dans l'encadrement d'une fenêtre,
une femme hésite . . . , pour être
celle que nous perdons
en l'ayant vue apparaître.

Et si elle lève les bras
pour nouer ses cheveux, tendre vase:
combien notre perte par là
gagne soudain d'emphase
et notre malheur d'éclat!

Your Invitation

You ask me to wait, strange window;
your beige curtain almost moves.
What should I do with your invitation,
accept it, resist? Who would I be waiting for?

Am I not intact, with a life that listens,
with this heart brimming over, completed by loss?
With this road that beckons, and the doubt
that, if I stayed, you'd give me what I dream of?

II

Tu me proposes, fenêtre étrange, d'attendre;
déjà presque bouge ton rideau beige.
Devrais-je, ô fenêtre, à ton invite me rendre?
Ou me défendre, fenêtre? Qui attendrais-je?

Ne suis-je intact, avec cette vie qui écoute,
avec ce cœur tout plein que la perte complète?
Avec cette route qui passe devant, et le doute
que tu puisses donner ce trop dont le rêve m'arrête?

Our Geometry

Window, are you not our geometry
whose simple shape circumscribes
effortlessly
this enormous life?

A lover is never so beautiful
as when she appears
in your frame, O window,
where she becomes almost immortal.

All danger is banished.
We cling to the center of love
surrounded by the only bit of space
we control.

III

N'es-tu pas notre géométrie,
fenêtre, très simple forme
qui sans effort circonscris
notre vie énorme?

Celle qu'on aime n'est jamais plus belle
que lorsqu'on la voit apparaître
encadrée de toi; c'est, ô fenêtre,
que tu la rends presque éternelle.

Tous les hasards sont abolis. L'être
se tient au milieu de l'amour,
avec ce peu d'espace autour
dont on est maître.

Measure of Longing

O window, measure of longing,
you refill so many times
as one life spills over and hurries
toward another life.

You who divide and who bring together,
as changeable as the sea,
a mirror, suddenly, reflecting and blending
our faces with what we see through you;

a glimpse of freedom compromised
by the presence of chance,
grasp that serves to balance out
the great excess of the world.

IV

Fenêtre, toi, ô mesure d'attente,
tant de fois remplie,
quand une vie se verse et s'impatiente
vers une autre vie.

Toi qui sépares et qui attires,
changeante comme la mer,—
glace, soudain, où notre figure se mire
mêlée à ce qu'on voit à travers;

échantillon d'une liberté compromise
par la présence du sort;
prise par laquelle parmi nous s'égalise
le grand trop du dehors.

You Make Ceremony

You make ceremony
of everything, window:
just standing in your frame
is to wait, or meditate.

You substantiate
the scattered, the lazy:
each looks the part a little,
resembles his reflection.

The child lost in boredom
leans against the pane,
dreaming. It's not his fault;
time wears out his sweater.

And we see our lovers,
motionless and frail,
pierced like butterflies
for the beauty of their wings.

V

Comme tu ajoutes à tout,
fenêtre, le sens de nos rites:
quelqu'un qui ne serait que debout,
dans ton cadre attend ou médite.

Tel distrait, tel paresseux,
c'est toi qui le mets en page:
il se ressemble un peu,
il devient son image.

Perdu dans un vague ennui,
l'enfant s'y appuie et reste;
il rêve . . . Ce n'est pas lui,
c'est le temps qui use sa veste.

Et les amantes, les y voit-on,
immobiles et frêles,
percées comme les papillons
pour la beauté de leurs ailes.

From the Bed

From the bed at the back of the room, a slight pallor separates
the retreat of the starry window from the greedy one
that announces the day.
Here she is, running, pushing forward, insisting.
After the night's abandon, this celestial youth
takes her turn to say *yes!*

Nothing but the morning sky for a sweet lover to contemplate,
nothing but itself, this sky, vast template
of depth and height!
Except for the doves' arenas in the air, gentle circles
of luminous flight that herald
a return to sweetness.

VI

Du fond de la chambre, du lit, ce n'était que pâleur qui sépare,
la fenêtre stellaire cédant à la fenêtre avare
qui proclame le jour.
Mais la voici qui accourt, qui se penche, qui reste:
après l'abandon de la nuit, cette neuve jeunesse céleste
consent à son tour!

Rien dans le ciel matinal que la tendre amante contemple,
rien que lui-même, ce ciel, immense exemple:
profondeur et hauteur!
Sauf les colombes qui font dans l'air de rondes arènes,
où leur vol allumé en douces courbes promène
un retour de douceur.

We Count on You

Window, we count on you
to add to the calculated room
the big wild numbers
multiplied by night.

Window where once a woman
sat disguised in sweetness
slowly doing her demeaning
and paralyzing work.

Window from whose carafe
images we've drunk will grow.
Clasp that buckles shut
the vast belt of our view.

VII

Fenêtre, qu'on cherche souvent
pour ajouter à la chambre comptée
tous les grands nombres indomptés
que la nuit va multipliant.

Fenêtre, où autrefois était assise
celle qui, en guise de tendresse,
faisait un lent travail qui baisse
et immobilise . . .

Fenêtre, dont une image bue
dans la claire carafe germe.
Boucle qui ferme
la vaste ceinture de notre vue.

Anxious Hours

She passes anxious hours
at the very edge of her being,
pressed against her window,
distracted and tense.

The greyhound, lying down,
carefully arranges its paws;
so too, her dream instinct takes over,
arranges the beauty

that is her perfectly positioned hands.
Everything else falls in line.
Not arm or breast, not shoulder,
not even the woman says: enough!

VIII

Elle passe des heures émues
appuyée à sa fenêtre,
toute au bord de son être,
distraite et tendue.

Comme les lévriers en
se couchant leurs pattes disposent,
son instinct de rêve surprend
et règle ces belles choses

que sont ses mains bien placées.
C'est par là que le reste s'enrôle.
Ni les bras, ni les seins, ni l'épaule,
ni elle-même ne disent: assez!

My Whole Abyss

When I saw you lean
out the ultimate window,
I knew I would drink
my whole abyss.

When you showed me your arms
reaching toward night,
you made the part of me
that left you
leave myself and flee . . . .

Did your farewell gesture
prove so grand
that it turned me to wind,
poured me in the river?

X

C'est pour t'avoir vue
penchée à la fenêtre ultime,
que j'ai compris, que j'ai bu
tout mon abîme.

En me montrant tes bras
tendus vers la nuit,
tu as fait que, depuis,
ce qui en moi te quitta,
me quitte, me fuit . . . .

Ton geste, fut-il la preuve
d'un adieu si grand,
qu'il me changea en vent,
qu'il me versa dans le fleuve?

Vertical Plate

Vertical plate serving us
the pittance that pursues us,
and the night too sweet,
and the day, often too bitter.

This never-ending meal
seasoned with blue—
we mustn't let ourselves go
and eat with our eyes alone.

So many dishes are offered
as the plums are ripening.
O my eyes, you've eaten roses,
now you'll drink the moon!

XI

Assiette verticale qui nous sert
la pitance qui nous poursuit,
et la trop douce nuit
et le jour, souvent trop amer.

L'interminable repas,
assaisonné de bleu—,
il ne faut pas être las
et se nourrir par les yeux.

Que de mets l'on nous propose
pendant que mûrissent les prunes;
ô mes yeux, mangeurs de roses,
vous allez boire la lune!

I'm in a Window Mood

I'm in a window mood today—
life seems to consist of simply looking.
I'm surprised by all the harmony I see,
intelligence as great as in a book.

Each bird that reaches into my view
with its flight asks for my consent.
And I give it. Inconsistency
used to terrify, now it comforts me.

You might find me in the middle of the night
having spent probably the entire day
surrendering to the inexhaustible window,
trying to be the other half of the world.

XII

Ce jour je suis d'humeur fenestrière,
rien que de regarder me semble vivre.
Tout me surprend d'un goût complémentaire,
d'intelligence plein comme dans un livre.

Chaque oiseau qui de son vol traverse
mon étendue, veut que je consente.
Et je consens. La force inconstante
ne m'épouvante plus, car elle me berce.

Me trouvera-t-on lorsque la nuit abonde
ayant passé le jour entier peut-être
livré à toi, inépuisable fenêtre,
pour être l'autre moitié du monde.

She Was in a Window Mood

She was in a window mood that day—
life seemed to consist of simply looking.
She watched the world emerge from chaos
and harmonize with her heart.

One could say that her gaze showered
abundant sweetness on the garden.
Was it freedom or bondage that prevented her
from changing her languid pose?

Her heart, far from the comings and goings,
could have been a number suddenly lit,
resembling Libra or the Lyre,
an almost-name for a thousand losses.

XIII

Ce jour elle fut d'humeur fenestrière:
rien que de regarder lui semblait vivre.
Elle vit venir, d'inexistence ivre,
un monde à son cœur complémentaire.

On aurait dit que son regard arrose
abondamment un doux jardin d'images;
était-ce liberté ou esclavage
de ne pas changer l'indolente pose?

Son cœur, loin de ce qui vit et vire,
semblait un nombre qui soudain s'éclaire
pareil à la Balance ou la Lyre;
un presque-nom d'absences millénaires.

How Long Have We Played You

How long have we played you,
window, with our eyes!
Like the lyre, you should be sent
to join the constellations.

Instrument gentle and strong
of our evolving souls,
deliver us now from the fate
of your unchanging shape.

Climb high and far!
Revolve around us who made you.
Be, heavenly bodies, the poems
of our destiny's end.

XV

Depuis quand nous te jouons
avec nos yeux, fenêtre!
Comme la lyre, tu devais être
rendue aux constellations!

Instrument tendre et fort
de nos âmes successives,
arrache enfin de nos sorts
ta forme définitive!

Monte! Tourne de loin
autour de nous qui te fîmes.
Soyez, astres, les rimes
trouvées à nos bouts de destin!

3

Affectionate Tribute to France

We must try to achieve the fullest consciousness of our existence, which is at
home in the two unseparated realms . . . . there is neither a here nor a beyond,
but great unity.[4]

Rilke wrote that his French verse served as a modest tribute not only to
Switzerland, but also "to France and to Paris the incomparable, which
for my development and in my memory signify a whole world."[5]

"Affectionate Tribute to France" is a short collection of thoughts, con-
fessions and supplications. When Rilke wrote these verses, he was already
beginning to feel the symptoms of his illness. In *The Sleeper*, the poet prays
that differences between war and peace, laughter and tears, masculine and
feminine, be blurred.

The odd pair in the center of the series, *L'Indifferent*—which is the title
of a painting by the rococo artist Watteau—and *Prayer of One Not Indif-
ferent Enough*, offer a darkly humorous contrast between the shallow life
of a socialite and the introverted existence of the sensitive, solitary artist.
This series depicts a poet who is "so easily hurt," acutely feels the death of
a child, and concludes, very softly, that our striving, studded with mistakes
like nuggets of gold, will probably have been worth all our effort in the end.

This is also the master poet who, in the end, doubts himself and his
contribution. I have chosen a phrase from the thirteenth poem of this series

4. Rainer Maria Rilke, *Sonnets to Orpheus*, trans. M. D. Herter Norton (New York:
Norton, 1942), 132.

5. Donald Prater, *A Ringing Glass*, (New York: Oxford University Press, 1986), 388.

for the title of this book because I find his question so moving and impor-
tant: "When I go, will I have spoken / this tormented heart that agrees to go
on?" What self-reflecting person in today's world has not asked this?

Tendres Impôts à la France (literally *"Tender Taxes to France"*) were
found among Rilke's papers and published posthumously.

The Sleeper

Leave me be . . . sleep is the truce
promised the sleeper between never-ending battles.
I wait and watch for the moon to rise
in my heart, where somber skies are clearing.

O temporary death, devastating sweetness,
you know how high I go and how deep,
the limbs of all my blood, the innocence of sap.
Even the root of my fear fears you not.

Sweet Lord of Slumber, deliver me from dreams
and mingle my laughter with my tears;
leave me ill-defined, so my inner Eve
won't feel tempted to tear out of my side.

i Le Dormeur

Laissez-moi dormir, encore . . . c'est la trêve
pendant de longs combats promise au dormeur,
je guette dans mon cœur la lune qui se lève,
bientôt il ne fera plus si sombre dans mon cœur.

Ô mort provisoire, douceur qui nous achève,
mesure de mes cimes, très juste profondeur,
limbes de tout mon sang, et innocence des sèves,
dans toi, à sa racine, ma peur même n'est pas peur.

Mon doux seigneur Sommeil, ne faites pas que je rêve
et mêlez en moi mes ris avec mes pleurs;
laissez-moi diffus, pour que l'interne Ève
ne sorte de mon flanc en son hostile ardeur.

Pegasus

Fiery white horse, Pegasus bright and proud,
how I love to see you halt after galloping!
You suddenly rear up, and where the trampled ground
swallows your flame, water flows.

The spring under your commanding hoof
brings welcome relief from our long, dry days.
Can you yourself feel the power of its sweetness?
Your vigorous neck curves like a flower.

2 PÉGASE

Cheval ardent et blanc, fier et clair Pégase,
après ta course—ah! que ton arrêt est beau!
Sous toi, cabré soudain, le sol que tu écrases
avale l'étincelle et donne de l'eau.

La source qui jaillit sous ton sabot dompteur,
à nous, qui l'attendons, est d'un secours suprême;
sens-tu que sa douceur impose à toi-même?
Car ton cou vigoureux apprend la courbe des fleurs.

The Magi

What could the three
Magi have brought?
A little bird in a cage,
an enormous key

to their far-away kingdom—
the third one a salve
his mother had made
of rare lavender

from their country.
There's no belittling this
for it was enough to turn
the child into God.

3
Qu'est-ce que les Rois Mages
ont-ils pu apporter?
Un petit oiseau dans sa cage,
une énorme clef

de leur lointain royaume—
et le troisième du baume
que sa mère avait préparé
d'une étrange lavande

de chez eux.
Faut pas médire de si peu
puisque ça suffit à l'enfant
pour devenir Dieu.

Stillness

Let's stay by the lamp and let words be few;
the experience of silence holds more promise
than anything we could say. Like the hollow
of a divine hand. True,
that hand is empty,
but a hand never opens in vain,
and a hand is what brings us together.

Not like ours: we hurry
slow things. Simply opening is
action for a hand. See
how it teems with life.
Strength comes with stillness;
let's relish this wordless peace
before power stirs again.

5

Restons à la lampe et parlons peu;
tout ce qu'on peut dire ne vaut pas l'aveu
du silence vécu; c'est comme le creux
d'une main divine.
Elle est vide, certes, la main, cette main;
mais une main ne s'ouvre jamais en vain,
et c'est elle qui nous combine.

Ce n'est pas la nôtre: nous précipitons
les choses lentes. C'est déjà l'action
qu'une main qui se montre. Regardons
la vie qui en elle afflue.

Celui qui bouge n'est pas le plus fort.
Il faut admirer son tacite accord
avant que la force remue.

"L'Indifférent" (Watteau)

Oh, to be born ardent and sad,
yet summoned to a genteel life,
to attend, well-dressed,
the many gay occasions

that don't concern you at all.
To be the charmer who aims
a smile at the charmed
from far across the room.

6 "L'INDIFFÉRENT" (WATTEAU)

Ô naître ardent et triste,
mais, à la vie convoqué,
être celui qui assiste,
tendre et bien habillé,

à la multiple surprise
qui ne vous engage point,
et, bien mis, à la bien mise
sourire de très loin.

Prayer of One Not Indifferent Enough

Help the hearts, so yielding and tender,
so easily hurt!
Who knows how to defend tenderness
from tenderness.

Yet the moon, a clement goddess,
never hurts anyone.
From falling unendingly into our sorrow,
save the moon!

7 Prière de la Trop Peu Indifférente

Aidez les cœurs, si soumis et si tendres—
tout cela blesse!
Qui saurait bien la tendresse défendre
de la tendresse.

Pourtant la lune, clémente déesse,
ne blesse aucune.
Ah, de nos pleurs où elle tombe sans cesse,
sauvez la lune!

All Must Be Well

All must be well if so much calm
follows such a storm. Life sings us
like a prelude, but the most surprising lines
of music sometimes belong to us
as much as to their instrument.

That unknown hand . . . is it happy, at least,
when it manages a melody on our strings?
Or have we forced that hand to insert
the denial of all our goodbyes
between the notes of our lullabies?

9

Il faut croire que tout est bien, si tant
de calme suit à tant d'inquiétude;
la vie, à nous, se passe en prélude,
mais parfois le chant qui nous surprend
nous appartient, comme à son instrument.

Main inconnue . . . . Au moins est-elle heureuse,
lorsqu'elle parvient à rendre mélodieuses
nos cordes?—Ou l'a-t-on forcée
de mêler même aux sons de la berceuse
tous les adieux inavoués?

Evening Lamp

Evening lamp, quiet companion,
you can't illuminate my heart;
it's a space we could get lost in,
but the south-facing slope is softly lit.

Lamp, you're still the one
who wants the reader, now and then,
to stop reading, adjust himself
over his book, and look at you with amazement.

(Your simplicity surpasses an Angel.)

II

Lampe du soir, ma calme confidente,
mon cœur n'est point par toi dévoilé;
on s'y perdrait peut-être; mais sa pente
du côté sud est doucement éclairée.

C'est encore toi, ô lampe d'étudiant,
qui veut que le liseur de temps en temps
s'arrête étonné et se dérange
sur son bouquin, te regardant.

(Et ta simplicité supprime un Ange.)

Lovers and Writers

Sometimes lovers or writers
find a few ephemeral words
that turn the heart into a glad place
of endless reverie. . . .

Invisible strength is born there
beneath everything that happens;
its footprints can't be seen
except in the steps of a dance.

12

Parfois les amants ou ceux qui écrivent
trouvent des mots qui, bien qu'ils s'effacent,
laissent dans un cœur une place heureuse
à jamais pensive . . . .

Car il en naît sous tout ce qui passe
d'invisibles persévérances;
sans qu'ils creusent aucune trace
quelques-uns restent des pas de la danse.

When I Go

When I go, will I have spoken
my tormented heart that agrees to go on?
Until my dying day must I learn from
that old teacher named Unexpected?

Words of tender admiration spoken too late
are eclipsed by a summer day.
Which of our half-open flower-words
exhale pure perfume?

And shouldn't this beautiful woman
step into a pastoral scene when she goes?
The sweet ribbon fluttering behind her
has more life than this grasping line.

13

L'aurai-je exprimé, avant de m'en aller,
ce cœur qui, tourmenté, consent à être?
Étonnement sans fin, qui fus mon maître,
jusqu'à la fin t'aurai-je imité?

Mais tout surpasse comme un jour d'été
le tendre geste qui trop tard admire;
dans nos paroles écloses, qui respire
le pur parfum d'identité?

Et cette belle qui s'en va, comment
la ferait-on passer par une image?
Son doux ruban flottant vit davantage
que cette ligne qui s'éprend.

The Grave

(in a park)

Sleep, child, under your stone
down at the end of the lane.
We'll circle around your empty space
and sing a summer song.

If a snow-white dove in flight
passes over our heads,
I can offer your grave only this:
its shadow as it falls.

14 Tombeau

[dans un parc]

Dors au fond de l'allée,
tendre enfant, sous la dalle;
on fera le chant de l'été
autour de ton intervalle.

Si une blanche colombe
passait au vol là-haut,
je n'offrirais à ton tombeau
que son ombre qui tombe.

What Longing, What Regret

To what longing, to what regret
have we fallen victim,
we who mine poetry
for the unique universal?

Obstinate that we are,
we let our mistakes lead the way,
but of all human mistakes,
that one is pure gold.

15
De quelle attente, de quel
regret sommes-nous les victimes,
nous qui cherchons des rimes
à l'unique universel?

Nous poursuivons notre tort
en obstinés que nous sommes;
mais entre les torts des hommes
c'est un tort tout en or.

4

Valaisian Quatrains

"I would describe myself
like a landscape I've studied
at length."[6]

Rilke considered these the core of his French poems.[7] Beyond the trib-ute to France, Switzerland, and the French language, the "Quatrains" express the spiritual aspect of the landscape of the Valais that had received him so well, where his soul had found solace.

Well grounded in geography and history, this place "Instead of deny-ing its nature, / . . . gives itself permission" to be itself, a land of natural paradox. In the interplay between light and shadow, soil and sun, there is dynamic alchemy that "will end up in the wine." Indeed, man-made influ-ence plays a seamless part in this landscape, especially the vineyards that produce "the cluster, the link / between us and the dead." Stone towers and their bells, crumbling walls overgrown with hedges, even the villages them-selves bless humanity with their teachings about memory and imperma-nence, embodying the essence of the earth, the same as any tree or stream.

I experience these poems like a Cezanne still-life, a study in con-trast with corners of darkness worth exploring and occasional bursts of bright color, reminders of goodness. Unlike a still-life, there is movement

6. Rainer Maria Rilke, *Rilke's Book of Hours,* trans. Anita Barrows and Joanna Macy (New York: Penguin, 2005), 69.

7. Liselotte Dieckmann, "Rainer Maria Rilke's French Poems," *Modern Language Quarterly,* 12 (1951) 323.

everywhere, the "gorgeous momentum" of the artisan. Often the reader's attention is directed upward, away from "this ardent land" to "climb toward a sky that nobly understands / its difficult past." Much spaciousness is revealed in the emptiness of sky and wind that "takes brightness / from tall cornstalks. . . / rising to higher altitudes." The marriage of solid earth with "all the youth of the sky" is the primordial source of creation in which artists of all time participate. In the sound of flowing water and the vineyards "in line," Rilke saw space in language, the silence "between words / moving along in rhythm."

Dramatic days of cloud-play lead to rest, as "evening settles / into infinite peace." Did Rilke find some of that peace within himself? He wrote in a letter that the hills of the Valais seemed to have space around them and bring space with them, like a Rodin sculpture. "It is not only the loveliest landscape I have ever seen, but capable of reflecting one's inner experience."[8]

8. Dieckmann, "Rainer Maria Rilke's French Poems," 331.

This Land

This land floats in mid-air
between earth and heaven,
with voices of water and stone,
young and old, gentle and strong

like an offering lifted
toward receiving hands.
Land at its best,
warm as fresh bread.

2

Pays, arrêté à mi-chemin
entre la terre et les cieux,
aux voix d'eau et d'airain,
doux et dur, jeune et vieux,

comme une offrande levé
vers accueillantes mains,
beau pays achevé
chaud comme le pain!

Rose and Wall

Lighted rose, a crumbling wall—
yet, on the slope of the hill
this high flower, like Proserpina,
makes a hesitant gesture.

The vineyard, no doubt, drinks its fill
of shadow, and too much light
gallops down upon it
from the wrong direction.

3
Rose de lumière, un mur qui s'effrite—
mais, sur la pente de la colline,
cette fleur qui, haute, hésite
dans son geste de Proserpine.

Beaucoup d'ombre entre sans doute
dans la sève de cette vigne;
et ce trop de clarté qui trépigne
au-dessus d'elle, trompe la route.

Towers

The towers of this ancient country insist
that their bells remember—
without being sad, the wrinkled features
sadly show their ancient shadows.

So many forces exhaust themselves:
sun turns the vineyards gold . . .
and spaces glimmer in the distance
like futures we do not know.

4

Contrée ancienne, aux tours qui insistent
tant que les carillons se souviennent—
aux regards qui, sans être tristes,
tristement montrent leurs ombres anciennes.

Vignes où tant de forces s'épuisent
lorsqu'un soleil terrible les dore . . .
Et, au loin, ces espaces qui luisent
comme des avenirs qu'on ignore.

Lovely Curve

Lovely curve along the ivy,
languid lane that slows the goats;
beautiful light that any jeweler
would wish to contain in a stone.

A poplar in its proper place
balances its verticality
with slow, solid green
that stretches from side to side.

5
Douce courbe le long du lierre,
chemin distrait qu'arrêtent des chèvres;
belle lumière qu'un orfèvre
voudrait entourer d'une pierre.

Peuplier, à sa place juste,
qui oppose sa verticale
à la lente verdure robuste
qui s'étire et qui s'étale.

Silent Land of Quiet Prophets

Silent land of quiet prophets,
    land that grows its wine,
where the hills still feel Genesis
    and never fear demise!

Land too proud to want to change,
    that, like elm and walnut,
obeys the coming of summer,
    happy to repeat itself.

Only water brings news to this land,
    all the generous waters
that soften the earth's hard consonants
    with their bright, clear vowels.

6

Pays silencieux dont les prophètes se taisent,
    pays qui prépare son vin;
où les collines sentent encore la Genèse
    et ne craignent pas la fin!

Pays, trop fier pour désirer ce qui transforme,
    qui, obéissant à l'été,
semble, autant que le noyer et que l'orme,
    heureux de se répéter.

Pays dont les eaux sont presque les seules nouvelles,
    toutes ces eaux qui se donnent,
mettant partout la clarté de leurs voyelles
    entre tes dures consonnes!

Alpine Meadows

Do you see the angelic alpine meadows
 high between the dark pines?
So distant, almost heavenly,
 lit with the strangest light.

From the bright valley all the way to the peaks,
 what airborne treasure!
Everything floating in this air
 will end up in the wine.

7

Vois-tu, là-haut, ces alpages des anges
 entre les sombres sapins?
Presque célestes, à la lumière étrange,
 ils semblent plus que loin.

Mais dans la claire vallée et jusqu'aux crêtes,
 quel trésor aérien!
Tout ce qui flotte dans l'air et qui s'y reflète
 entrera dans ton vin.

The Invisible

It's almost the invisible that glimmers
above the winged incline;
a bit of clear night lingers
mingled with the silver of day.

Look, the light is so light
on the long-suffering contours,
and the hamlets down there, someone
consoles them for being so far away.

9

C'est presque l'invisible qui luit
au-dessus de la pente ailée;
il reste un peu d'une claire nuit
à ce jour en argent mêlée.

Vois, la lumière ne pèse point
sur ces obéissants contours,
et, là-bas, ces hameaux, d'être loin,
quelqu'un les console toujours.

Altars Where the Fruit Was Laid

Oh, these altars where the fruit was laid
alongside a lovely terebinth branch
or one from the pale olive tree—
and also a flower, dying, bruised in an embrace.

Hidden in the green of this vineyard,
could we find the original altar?
The offering is ripe; the Virgin herself
would bless it, counting her carillon beads.

10

Ô ces autels où l'on mettait des fruits
avec un beau rameau de térébinthe
ou de ce pâle olivier—et puis
la fleur qui meurt, écrasée par l'étreinte.

Entrant dans cette vigne, trouverait-on
l'autel naïf, caché par la verdure?
La Vierge même bénirait la mûre
offrande, égrainant son carillon.

This Sanctuary

Even so, let us bring to this sanctuary
all that nourishes—bread and salt,
these handsome grapes—and bewilder the mother
with this immense maternal realm.

Across the ages, this chapel has linked
ancient gods with gods of the future,
and this ancient, wise walnut tree
offers its shade, a pure temple.

II

Portons quand même à ce sanctuaire
tout ce qui nous nourrit: le pain, le sel,
ce beau raisin . . . . Et confondons la mère
avec l'immense règne maternel.

Cette chapelle, à travers les âges,
relie d'anciens dieux aux dieux futurs,
et l'ancien noyer, cet arbre-mage,
offre son ombre comme un temple pur.

The Belltower Sings

I'm not an ordinary tower.
I warm my carillon to make it ready.
May it be sweet, may it be good
for the Valaisian women.

Every Sunday, note by note,
I scatter my manna among them.
Let my carillon be good
for the Valaisian women.

May it be sweet, may it be good
on Saturday night in the towns
when the droplets of carillon fall
on the men of the Valaisian women.

12: Le Clocher Chante

Mieux qu'une tour profane,
je me chauffe pour mûrir mon carillon.
Qu'il soit doux, qu'il soit bon
aux Valaisannes.

Chaque dimanche, ton par ton,
je leur jette ma manne;
qu'il soit bon, mon carillon,
aux Valaisannes.

Qu'il soit doux, qu'il soit bon;
samedi soir dans les channes
tombe en gouttes mon carillon
aux Valaisans des Valaisannes.

The Year Turns

The year turns on the pivot
of peasant perseverance;
the Virgin and Saint Anne
both have something to say.

More ancient words
also come into play;
everything is blessed
and out of the earth

comes a timid green
whose effort eventually
yields the cluster, the link
between us and the dead.

13

L'année tourne autour du pivot
de la constance paysanne;
la Vierge et Sainte Anne
disent chacune leur mot.

D'autres paroles s'ajoutent
plus anciennes encor—
elles bénissent toutes,
et de la terre sort

cette verdure soumise
qui, par un long effort,
donne la grappe prise
entre nous et les morts.

A Rosy Mauve

A rosy mauve in the tall grass,
a gentle gray, the vineyards in line . . .
but a glorious sky above the slopes
looks like a prince who's receiving.

This ardent land nobly climbs
toward a sky that nobly understands
that a difficult past forever requires
a life of vigor and vigilance.

14

Un rose mauve dans les hautes herbes,
un gris soumis, la vigne alignée . . . .
Mais au-dessus des pentes, la superbe
d'un ciel qui reçoit, d'un ciel princier.

Ardent pays qui noblement s'étage
vers ce grand ciel qui noblement comprend
qu'un dur passé à tout jamais s'engage
à être vigoureux et vigilant.

Yesteryear

Everything sings of yesteryear,
but not in a way that destroys tomorrow;
we can feel the valiant, primordial power
in sky and wind, bread and hand.

It's not a past that colors everything
or fixes in place these ancient shapes.
It's the earth, pleased with her reflection
and consenting to her first day.

15

Tout ici chante la vie de naguère,
non pas dans un sens qui détruit le demain;
on devine, vaillants, dans leur force première
le ciel et le vent, et la main et le pain.

Ce n'est point un hier qui partout se propage
arrêtant à jamais ces anciens contours:
c'est la terre contente de son image
et qui consent à son premier jour.

How Calm the Night

How calm the night, how calm
the penetrating sky.
As though in your palm it were tracing
again the first design.

The little fountain sings
to hide its excited nymph. . . .
One feels the emptiness
that space is drinking in.

16

Quel calme nocturne, quel calme
nous pénètre du ciel.
On dirait qu'il refait dans la palme
de vos mains le dessin essentiel.

La petite cascade chante
pour cacher sa nymphe émue . . . .
On sent la présence absente
que l'espace a bue.

Everything Changes

Before you can count to ten
everything changes:
the wind takes brightness
from tall cornstalks

and flings it away;
it flies and slides
along a precipice
toward a sister brightness

that in turn is swept
into this boisterous game,
rising
to higher altitudes.

This vast landscape
may have been shaped
by these enchantments,
these gestures like caresses.

17

Avant que vous comptiez dix
tout change: le vent ôte
cette clarté des hautes
tiges de maïs,

pour la jeter ailleurs;
elle vole, elle glisse
le long d'un précipice
vers une clarté-sœur

qui déjà, à son tour,
prise par ce jeu rude,
se déplace pour
d'autres altitudes.

Et comme caressée
la vaste surface reste
éblouie sous ces gestes
qui l'avaient peut-être formée.

Serious Darkness

Such serious darkness
makes the mountain seem older;
it's an ancient land indeed
that counts Saint Charlemagne

among its paternal saints.
Yet, from high above,
carrying its own secret,
comes all the youth of the sky.

19

Tant de noir sérieux
rend plus âgée la montagne;
c'est bien ce pays très vieux
qui compte Saint Charlemagne

parmi ses saints paternels.
Mais par en haut lui viennent,
à la secrète sienne,
toutes les jeunesses du ciel.

Clematis and Morning Glory

The little clematis abandons
her hold on the tangled hedge
and the white morning glory waits
for her time to close up again.

They form bouquets
along the lane where berries redden.
Already? Is summer over?
The accomplice it chooses is autumn.

20

La petite clématite se jette
en dehors de la haie embrouillée
avec ce liseron blanc qui guette
le moment de se refermer.

Cela forme le long du chemin
des bouquets où des baies rougissent.
Déjà? Est-ce que l'été est plein?
Il prend l'automne pour complice.

After a Day of Wind

After a day of wind,
the evening settles
into infinite peace
like a docile lover.

All is calm and clear . . .
but on the horizon,
brightly lit in gold,
steps of clouds in bas-relief.

2 1

Après une journée de vent,
dans une paix infinie,
le soir se réconcilie
comme un docile amant.

Tout devient calme, clarté . . .
Mais à l'horizon s'étage,
éclairé et doré,
un beau bas-relief de nuages.

The Astonishment of Origins

One who speaks of his mother
begins to resemble her,
just as this land becomes itself
by remembering, always.

Just as the shoulders of these hills
surrender to the first movement
of this pure space that returns them
to the astonishment of origins.

2 2

Comme tel qui parle de sa mère
lui ressemble en parlant,
ce pays ardent se désaltère
en se souvenant infiniment.

Tant que les épaules des collines
rentrent sous le geste commençant
de ce pur espace qui les rend
à l'étonnement des origines.

Earth's Role

All around this place
there's evidence of earth's role
as a star. Gentle and humble,
she wears her aureole.

When our eyes launch out
into these pure distances,
you'd need a nightingale's voice
to measure it!

23

Ici la terre est entourée
de ce qui convient à son rôle
d'astre; tendrement humiliée,
elle porte son auréole.

Lorsqu'un regard s'élance: quel vol
par ces distances pures;
il faut la voix du rossignol
pour en prendre mesure.

The Silvering Hour

Here again is the silvering hour,
precious metal melting into evening,
adding to the slow beauty
slow refrains of quiet music.

This ancient earth, a star so pure,
changes, recovers, survives our labors.
Scattered noises leave the day,
arrange themselves in the voice of water.

24

Voici encor de l'heure qui s'argente,
mêlé au doux soir, le pur métal
et qui ajoute à la beauté lente
les lents retours d'un calme musical.

L'ancienne terre se reprend et change:
un astre pur survit à nos travaux.
Les bruits épars, quittant le jour, se rangent
et rentrent tous dans la voix des eaux.

Green

Along the dusty lane
the green is almost gray;
but that gray, subdued,
is laced with silver and blue.

Higher, on another plane,
a willow flashes the bright back
of its fluttering leaves
against a greenish black.

And over there, a green so casual,
a pale, ethereal green
that wildly encircles the tower
the century is breaking down.

25

Le long du chemin poussiéreux
le vert se rapproche du gris;
mais ce gris, quoique soumis,
contient de l'argent et du bleu.

Plus haut, sur un autre plan,
un saule montre le clair
revers de ses feuilles au vent
devant un noir presque vert.

À côté, un vert tout abstrait,
un pale vert de vision,
entoure d'un fond d'abandon
la tour que le siècle défait.

The Towers Remember

These towers crumble with dignity,
all the while remembering
their aerial life
from way back when.

The long relationship
with penetrating light
slows their matter down
and strengthens their decline.

26

Fier abandon de ces tours
qui pourtant se souviennent—
depuis quand jusqu'à toujours—
de leur vie aérienne.

Cet innombrable rapport
avec la clarté pénétrante
rend leur matière plus lente
et leur déclin plus fort.

Hard and Soft

Hard by nature are the towers,
thatched cottages, walls,
even the soil prepared
for the vineyard's joy.

But the light imposes softness
on this austerity,
lends the texture of peaches
to all these satisfied things.

27

Les tours, les chaumières, les murs,
même ce sol qu'on désigne
au bonheur de la vigne,
ont le caractère dur.

Mais la lumière qui prêche
douceur à cette austérité
fait une surface de pêche
à toutes ces choses comblées.

Song of Silence

A land that sings while working,
a land content to work;
waters sing their constant song,
the vineyard links its links.

A quiet land, for the waters' song
is nothing if not silence,
this silence, between words
moving along in rhythm.

28

Pays qui chante en travaillant,
pays heureux qui travaille;
pendant que les eaux continuent leur chant,
la vigne fait maille pour maille.

Pays qui se tait, car le chant des eaux
n'est qu'un excès de silence,
de ce silence entre les mots
qui, en rythmes, avancent.

The Artisan

The wind takes this land like an artisan
who's long known and used his medium;
it's warm and ready, he knows what to do,
and takes delight in his labor.

No one could stop his gorgeous momentum,
no one could oppose his outrageous fire—
but he's also the one who steps way back
as he holds up to his creation the clear mirror of space.

29

Vent qui prend ce pays comme l'artisan
qui, depuis toujours, connaît sa matière;
en la trouvant, toute chaude, il sait comment faire,
et il s'exalte en travaillant.

Nul n'arrêterait son élan magnifique; nul
ne saurait s'opposer à cette fougueuse audace—
et c'est encor lui qui, prenant un énorme recul,
tend à son oeuvre la clair miroir de l'espace.

Permission

Instead of denying its nature,
this land gives itself permission
to be both gentle and harsh,
threatened and redeemed.

Fervently it surrenders
to its inspiration, the sky;
the wind is aroused, pulling
toward it this light, new, fresh,

never before seen,
from beyond the mountains:
the horizon hesitates,
finally approaches her, leaping.

30

Au lieu de s'évader,
ce pays consent à lui-même;
ainsi il est doux et extrême,
menacé et sauvé.

Il s'adonne avec ferveur
à ce ciel qui l'inspire;
il excite son vent et attire
par lui la plus neuve primeur

de cette inédite
lumière d'outre-mont:
l'horizon qui hésite
lui arrive par bonds.

Lanes Leading Nowhere

Lanes between meadows,
leading nowhere,
as if directed away
from their goal by design,

lanes that often
look out on nothing
but pure space
and the season.

31

Chemins qui ne mènent nulle part
entre deux prés,
que l'on dirait avec art
de leur but détournés,

chemins qui souvent n'ont
devant eux rien d'autre en face
que le pur espace
et la saison.

What Goddess, What God

What goddess, what god
gave itself to this place,
the better for us
to sense its clear face.

Divine particles
swirl and fill
and expand
this pure valley.

It loves, it sleeps.
We climb into its body,
the Caves of Sesame,
and sleep inside its soul.

32

Quelle déesse, quel dieu
s'est rendu à l'espace,
pour que nous sentions mieux
la clarté de sa face.

Son être dissous
remplit cette pure
vallée du remous
de sa vaste nature.

Il aime, il dort.
Forts du Sésame,
nous entrons dans son corps
et dormons dans son âme.

Blue Wind

Could it be that shepherds
and growers of wine,
eternally contemplating
and praising the sky,

keep it there
with their eyes,
this fair sky and its wind,
the blue wind?

And the calm that follows,
so heavy, so deep,
like a satisfied god
falling asleep.

33
Ce ciel qu'avaient contemplé
ceux qui le loueront
pendant l'éternité:
bergers et vignerons,

serait-il par leurs yeux
devenu permanent,
ce beau ciel et son vent,
son vent bleu?

Et son calme après,
si profond et si fort,
comme un dieu satisfait
qui s'endort.

Perfecting the Slow Face

Not only the gaze of those
who work the fields, but also
the gaze of the goats helps
to perfect the slow

face of the Noble Landscape.
We are always contemplating
this place as if we could stay
or fix it forever

in a memory so impressive
that even the angel seeking
more brilliance would never
dare intervene.

34

Mais non seulement le regard
de ceux qui travaillent les champs,
celui des chèvres prend part
à parfaire le lent

aspect de la Noble Contrée.
On la contemple toujours
comme pour y rester ou pour
l'éterniser

dans un si grand souvenir
qu'aucun ange n'osera,
pour augmenter son éclat,
intervenir.

A Story

The earth tells her story
to an eager sky,
memories that lifted and shaped her
into noble mountains.

At times she seems moved
to be so well listened to
so she reveals her life
and then falls silent.

35
Au ciel, plein d'attention,
ici la terre raconte;
son souvenir la surmonte
dans ces nobles monts.

Parfois elle paraît attendrie
qu'on l'écoute si bien—
alors elle montre sa vie
et ne dit plus rien.

Book of Flight

A lovely butterfly flying low
shows whatever is watching
the illuminations
in its book of flight.

Another one closes its wings
on the edge of a breathable flower;
this isn't the time for reading.
Still others scatter,

the essence of blue,
floating and fluttering away
like the wispy blue fragments
of a love letter in the wind,

the torn-up letter
that was just being written
while its addressee
stood in the door.

36

Beau papillon près du sol,
à l'attentive nature
montrant les enluminures
de son livre de vol.

Un autre se ferme au bord
de la fleur qu'on respire:
ce n'est pas le moment de lire.
Et tant d'autres encor,

de menus bleus, s'éparpillent,
flottant et voletant,
comme de bleues brindilles
d'une lettre d'amour au vent,

d'une lettre déchirée
qu'on était en train de faire
pendant que la destinataire
hésitait à l'entrée.

Valaisian Sky

Each beat of our hearts
desperately needs advice about balance,
the kind that's given
by the whole broad sky!

The sky has known
our sorrows forever;
it is a friend to the rugged earth,
smoothing out its edges.

37: CIEL VALAISAN

Comment notre cœur lorsqu'il vibre
a-t-il tant besoin
que tout un ciel de loin
lui donne des conseils d'équilibre.

Mais ce ciel depuis toujours
a de nos cris l'habitude;
ami de la terre rude,
il en adoucit le contour.

5

Orchards

"There is no difference between what is seen and the mind that sees it."[9]

Of "Orchards," Dieckmann writes: "[Rilke] begins to realize that his end is near. There is a difference between the acceptance of Death as part of life, such as Rilke had expressed it so often, and the clear realization that now his own death is near . . ."[10]

The title poem in this series of fifty-nine, *Orchard*, occurs in the middle of the series, like the fountain at the orchard's center, from which all else flows. Nature is depicted in the most subtle turns of phrase that result, somehow, in the impossibility of the reader to project himself into the "thing" described, e.g. tree or breeze. Yet, we are one with these phenomena. Rilke informs us that "orchard and road are no different / from anything we are."

The orchard is a container, a kind of hologram for all of life and its seasons, most especially the poignant decline at the turning from summer to autumn. The joy, magic and perfection of ripe fruit brings the end of a happy season. Summer, by definition, betrays us with its bright promises.

"I've said my goodbyes," Rilke declares in the last entry in the series. These poems, more than any other in this book, express Rilke's poetic farewell to his beloved world. He reckons with god, "the heavy hand of the Invisible," pleading, "May the god be satisfied / with our brief shining moment / before sending a malevolent wave / that smashes us to pieces."

9. Yongey Mingyur Rinpoche, *Joyful Wisdom* (New York: Three Rivers, 2009), 151.
10. Dieckmann, "Rainer Maria Rilke's French Poems," 336.

He points out, one last time, the importance of paradox: "It's natural for the Organ to growl / so that every note of music / can abound with love."

I don't know who he had in mind when he wrote "Elegy," but I think of his enduring spirit when I read it: "How many lives will continue to echo, / and given the altitude at which you flew / while in this world, / a great void is no longer so hollow."

Visitation

Stay calm if suddenly your table
is the one the Angel chooses.
Gently smooth the wrinkles
in the tablecloth under the bread.

Then offer him a taste
of your rustic food, let him
raise to his pure lips
a simple everyday cup.

3
Reste tranquille, si soudain
l'Ange à ta table se décide;
efface doucement les quelques rides
que fait la nappe sous ton pain.

Tu offriras ta rude nourriture
pour qu'il en goûte à son tour,
et qu'il soulève à sa lèvre pure
un simple verre de tous les jours.

Strange Assignment

What a strange assignment
have we whispered to the flowers,
to measure the weight of passion
with their delicate scales.

The stars are completely confused
when we involve them in our grief.
And nothing, from frail to strong,
has ever shown itself willing

to entertain our changing moods,
our impetuousness, our cries,
except the tireless table
and the table that's fainted, the bed.

4

Combien a-t-on fait aux fleurs
d'étranges confidences,
pour que cette fine balance
nous dise le poids de l'ardeur.

Les astres sont tous confus
qu'à nos chagrins on les mêle.
Et du plus fort au plus frêle
nul ne supporte plus

notre humeur variable,
nos révoltes, nos cris—
sauf l'infatigable table
et le lit (table évanouie).

The Hand of the Invisible

Who knows how much of us
he will refuse, the day we finally surrender
to the heavy hand of the Invisible
and his invisible ruse.

Our core eventually obeys our longing,
steps aside to allow the heart,
Grand Master of Loss,
to have its way.

6

Nul ne sait, combien ce qu'il refuse,
l'Invisible, nous domine, quand
notre vie à l'invisible ruse
cède, invisiblement.

Lentement, au gré des attirances
notre centre se déplace pour
que le cœur s'y rende à son tour:
lui, enfin Grand-Maître des absences.

Palm

For Mrs. and Mr. Albert Vulliez

The sleeping stars
have climbed skyward,
have left their soft
disheveled bed.

Was this a good bed?
Are they rested now,
clear and shiny,
swirling among
their fellow stars?

O these hands, two beds
abandoned and cold,
missing the solid weight
of those stars.

7: Paume

À Mme. et M. Albert Vulliez

Paume, doux lit froissé
òu des etoiles dormantes
avaient laissé des plis
en se levant vers le ciel.

Est-ce que ce lit était tel
qu'elles se trouvent reposées,

claires et incandescentes,
parmi les astres amis
en leur élan éternel?

Ô les deux lits de mes mains,
abandonnés et froids,
légers d'un absent poids
de ces astres d'airain.

The Last Word

Our next-to-last word
might be a word of misery,
but faced with Mother Conscience,
the last one will be lovely.

That word will return us
to the workings of a desire
that no hint of bitterness
knows how to overcome.

8

Notre avant-dernier mot
serait un mot de misère,
mais devant la conscience-mère
le tout dernier sera beau.

Car il faudra qu'on résume
tous les efforts d'un désir
qu'aucun goût d'amertume
ne saurait contenir.

The Exchange

If we sing a god,
only silence returns.
Our futures hold nothing
but silent gods.

Though we can't hear or see it,
this exchange shakes us;
it's the heritage of angels
never meant for us.

9

Si l'on chante un dieu,
ce dieu vous rend son silence.
Nul de nous ne s'avance
que vers un dieu silencieux.

Cet imperceptible échange
qui nous fait frémir,
devient l'héritage d'un ange
sans nous appartenir.

Venetian Glass

Venetian glass is born
knowing it will fall in love
with this shade of gray
and this vacillating light,

just as your tender hands
dreamed in advance
of slowing down
the intensity of our moments.

12

Comme un verre de Venise
sait en naissant ce gris
et la clarté indécise
dont il sera épris,

ainsi tes tendres mains
avaient rêvé d'avance
d'être la lente balance
de nos moments trop pleins.

A Summer Passerby

Do you see her there, the one we envy,
walking on the path, slow and happy?
At the turn in the road, handsome gentlemen
of days gone by ought to stop and greet her.

Under her parasol, with casual grace,
she avails herself of a gentler choice:
disappearing briefly in the blinding brightness,
she shines in the shade she brings with her.

14: La Passante d'Été

Vois-tu venir sur le chemin la lente, l'heureuse,
celle que l'on envie, la promeneuse?
Au tournant de la route il faudrait qu'elle soit
saluée par de beaux messieurs d'autrefois.

Sous son ombrelle, avec une grâce passive,
elle exploite la tendre alternative:
s'effaçant un instant à la trop brusque lumière,
elle ramène l'ombre dont elle s'éclaire.

The Whole Night

The whole night is lifted
on a lover's sigh,
one brief caress
across a dazzled sky.

As if in the universe
an elemental force
became again the mother
of all love lost.

15

Sur le soupire de l'amie
toute la nuit se soulève,
une caresse brève
parcourt le ciel ébloui.

C'est comme si dans l'univers
une force élémentaire
redevenait la mère
de tout amour qui se perd.

The Temple of Love

Who will help finish the temple of Love?
Each person brings one of the columns,
and when it's done the god will come
and breach the enclosure with his arrow.

We're shocked, and yet
that's his reputation.
Our cries grow like vines
on this wall of abandon.

17

Qui vient finir le temple de l'Amour?
Chacun en emporte une colonne;
et à la fin tout le monde s'étonne
que le dieu à son tour

de sa flèche brise l'enceinte.
(Tel nous le connaissons.)
Et sur ce mur d'abandon
pousse la plainte.

Water and Love

Water, how quickly you run away, forgetting,
blithely drunk by the earth.
Now linger in the cup of my hands for a moment
　　　　　　with your memories!

Love runs clear and bright, indifferent,
almost here but gone;
between too much arrival and too much parting
　　　　　　trembles a little sojourn.

18

Eau qui se presse, qui court—eau oublieuse
que la distraite terre boit,
hésite un petit instant dans ma main creuse,
　　　　　　souviens-toi!

Clair et rapide amour, indifférence,
presque absence qui court,
entre ton trop d'arrivée et ton trop de partance
　　　　　　tremble un peu de séjour.

Eros

I

You are the focus of a game
where winning means losing,
as famous as Charlemagne,
emperor, god, king—

and, you're the pitiful beggar
standing hunched on the corner:
it's your changeable face
that gives you such power.

This could all be good,
but it isn't: *in us* you're like
the black interior of an embroidered
cashmere shawl.

19: Eros

I

Ô toi, centre du jeu
où l'on perd quand on gagne;
célèbre comme Charlemagne,
roi, empereur et Dieu—

tu es aussi le mendiant
en pitoyable posture,
et c'est ta multiple figure
qui te rend puissant.

Tout ceci serait pour le mieux;
mais tu es, *en nous* (c'est pire),
comme le noir milieu
d'un châle brodé de cachemire.

II

In order for a fire so wild to be tamed,
we must risk everything, even danger
and disruption. His face must be obscured,
he must be returned to the beginning of time.

He comes in so close, he wedges himself
between us and the lover he claims as his own;
he wants our touch, this barbaric god
panthers brush against in the desert.

He enters us with his grand cortege,
expecting everything to be well lit.
Later he escapes as from a trap,
without having touched the bait.

II

Ô faisons tout pour cacher son visage
d'un mouvement hagard et hasardeux,
il faut le reculer au fond des âges
pour adoucir son indomptable feu.

Il vient si près de nous qu'il nous sépare
de l'être bien-aimé dont il se sert;
il veut qu'on touche; c'est un dieu barbare
que des panthères frôlent au désert.

Entrant en nous avec son grand cortège,
il y veut tout illuminé—
lui, qui, après se sauve comme d'un piège,
sans qu'aux appâts il ait touché.

III

Sometimes we spot him under the arbor,
there, deep in the foliage:
the ruddy face of that *enfant sauvage*,
his wrinkled, gnarly mouth. . . .

The grapes sag down in front of him,
heavy under their own tired weight;
for one terrifying moment we feel
how happily summer betrays us.

He proudly infuses all the fruits
with the raw color of his smile.
Then he uses the same old trick
to gently rock himself to sleep.

III

Là, sous la treille, parmi le feuillage
il nous arrive de le deviner:
son front rustique d'enfant sauvage,
et son antique bouche mutilée. . . .

La grappe devant lui devient pesante
et semble fatiguée de sa lourdeur,
un court moment on frôle l'épouvante
de cet heureux été trompeur.

Et son sourire cru, comme il l'infuse
à tous les fruits de son fier décor;
partout autour il reconnaît sa ruse
qui doucement le berce et l'endort.

IV

It isn't justice that balances the scales,
it's you, O God of undivided envy,
who weigh our mistakes.
You take two hearts, mash them to a pulp,
and make one immense preternatural heart
that wants to continue
to swell . . . . You, indifferent and superb,
humble the mouth and exalt the word
to an ignorant sky . . . .
You break apart the living and send
their fragments to the void where they belong.

IV

Ce n'est pas la justice qui tient la balance précise,
c'est toi, ô Dieu à l'envie indivise,
qui pèses nos torts,
et qui de deux cœurs qu'il meurtrit et triture
fais un immense cœur plus grand que nature,
qui voudrait encor
grandir . . . . Toi, qui indifférent et superbe,
humilies la bouche et exaltes le verbe
vers un ciel ignorant . . . .
Toi qui mutiles les êtres en les ajoutant
à l'ultime absence dont ils sont des fragments.

May the God Be Satisfied

May the god be satisfied
with our brief shining moment
before sending a malevolent wave
that smashes us to pieces.

There was a time when we saw eye to eye,
but he survived, persisted,
while our downcast hearts
were astonished at his energy.

20

Que le dieu se contente de nous,
de notre instant insigne,
avant qu'une vague maligne
nous renverse et pousse à bout.

Un moment nous étions d'accord:
lui, qui survit et persiste,
et nous dont le cœur triste
s'étonne de son effort.

What We Are

Let us recognize each nuance
of each thing we encounter,
so that, amidst randomness,
order will reveal itself.

What surrounds us wants to be heard.
Let's listen to the very end,
for orchard and road are no different
from anything we are!

2 1

Dans la multiple rencontre
faisons à tout sa part,
afin que l'ordre se montre
parmi les propos du hasard.

Tout autour veut qu'on l'écoute—
écoutons jusqu'au bout;
car le verger et la route
c'est toujours nous!

Equilibrium

By the sacred law of opposites
the pope, with all his pomp and finery,
attracts the devil
without being any less venerable.

We often forget that things
naturally find equilibrium.
The Tiber has its currents;
all play wants counter-play.

I remember Rodin one day
telling me in his cocky way
(we were leaving Chartres by train)
that, at its purest, the cathedral
stirs up a wind of disdain.

23
Combien le pape au fond de son faste,
sans être moins vénérable,
par la sainte loi du contraste
doit attirer le diable.

Peut-être qu'on compte trop peu
avec ce mouvant équilibre;
il y a des courants dans le Tibre:
tout jeu veut son contre-jeu.

Je me rappelle Rodin
qui me dit un jour d'un air mâle

(nous prenions, à Chartres, le train)
que, trop pure, la cathédrale
provoque un vent de dédain.

The Turn

We make a great show of repenting.
Still, we are much too proud.
If we surrendered
to all the strong forces,

what threatens us
would become changeable:
calm would turn to hurricane,
the abyss to an angel's crucible.

Don't be afraid of the turn.
It's natural for the Organ to growl
so that every note of music
can abound with love.

24

C'est qu'il nous faut consentir
à toutes les forces extrêmes;
l'audace est notre problème
malgré le grand repentir.

Et puis, il arrive souvent
que ce qu'on affronte, change:
le calme devient ouragan,
l'abîme le moule d'un ange.

Ne craignons pas le détour.
Il faut que les Orgues grondent,
pour que la musique abonde
de toutes les notes de l'amour.

We Forget

So often we forget
the gods' habit of fighting,
that we envy pious souls
their naïve proceedings.

Pleasing them or being converted
are both beside the point:
we must know how to obey
contradictory orders.

2 5

On a si bien oublié
les dieux opposés et leurs rites,
qu'on envie aux âmes confites
leur naïf procédé.

Il ne s'agit pas de plaire,
ni de se convertir,
pourvu que l'on sache obéir
aux ordres complémentaires.

The Fountain

Yours is the only lesson I want,
fountain, the one where you fall backward
into yourself, where everything is risked
on the celestial return to earth.

Nothing could serve as a better example
than the overtones in your murmur,
O weightless column of the temple,
who take yourself down by nature!

Each spout of water falls, and falling,
changes by the end of its dance.
I feel like a student trying to emulate
your richly layered nuance.

What moves me even more than your song
is that moment of delirious silence, at night,
when your headlong momentum stops itself
like an indrawn breath.

26: La Fontaine

Je ne veux qu'une seule leçon, c'est la tienne,
fontaine, qui en toi-même retombes—
celle des eaux risquées auxquelles incombe
ce céleste retour vers la vie terrienne.

Autant que ton multiple murmure
rien ne saurait me servir d'exemple;
toi, ô colonne légère du temple
qui se détruit par sa propre nature.

Dans ta chute, combien se module
chaque jet d'eau qui termine sa danse.
Que je me sens l'élève, l'émule
de ton innombrable nuance!

Mais ce qui plus que ton chant vers toi me décide
c'est cet instant d'un silence en délire
lorsqu'à la nuit, à travers ton élan liquide
passe ton propre retour qu'un souffle retire.

My Body

How sweet sometimes to agree with you,
O my body, my elder brother,
how sweet to be strong
with your strength,
to feel you, leaf, branch and bark
and all that you are still becoming,
you, so close to the spirit,

so free, so at one
with the obvious joy
of being this tree of gestures.
You slow heaven down
for a moment, and give it
a place to call home.

27

Qu'il est doux parfois d'être de ton avis,
frère aîné, ô mon corps,
qu'il est doux d'être fort
de ta force,
de te sentir feuille, tige, écorce
et tout ce que tu peux devenir encor,
toi, si près de l'esprit.

Toi, si franc, si uni
dans ta joie manifeste
d'être cet arbre de gestes
qui, un instant, ralentit
les allures célestes
pour y placer sa vie.

Verger [Orchard]

I

Perhaps, dear borrowed language,
I've been emboldened to use you because
of the rustic word whose unique domain
has taunted me forever: *Verger.*

Pity the poet who must settle for less
than this comprehensive word, choosing
between some vague, sinking equivalent,
and worse, an armed fortress.

Verger. Only a musical instrument
could utter such a simple word:
nectar to bees, a word without equal,
a word that breathes and waits,

big enough for the whole history of spring,
bright, dense and yet transparent,
a word whose symmetrical syllables
multiply out of sheer abundance.

29: VERGER

I

Peut-être que si j'ai osé t'écrire,
langue prêtée, c'était pour employer
ce nom rustique dont l'unique empire
me tourmentait depuis toujours: Verger.

Pauvre poète qui doit élire
pour dire tout ce que ce nom comprend,
un à peu près trop vague qui chavire,
ou pire: la clôture qui défend.

Verger: ô privilège d'une lyre
de pouvoir te nommer simplement;
nom sans pareil qui les abeilles attire,
nom qui respire et attend . . . .

Nom clair qui cache le printemps antique,
tout aussi plein que transparent,
et qui dans ses syllabes symétriques
redouble tout et devient abondant.

II

Which sun pulls
such heavy desire into its orbit?
This ardor you speak of,
where is its firmament?

Why do we struggle so
to feel one another's pleasure?
Let us all tread lightly.
The earth is already spinning
with too much enmity.

Take a good look at the orchard
with its undeniable heaviness.
From that malaise
comes the happiness of summer.

II

Vers quel soleil gravitent
tant de désirs pesants?
De cette ardeur que vous dites,
où est le firmament?

Pour l'un à l'autre nous plaire,
faut-il tant appuyer?
Soyons légers et légères
à la terre remuée
par tant de forces contraires.

Regardez bien le verger:
c'est inévitable qu'il pèse;
pourtant de ce même malaise
il fait le bonheur de l'été.

III

Earth was never so real
as in the light of your branches, O orchard,
and earth was never lighter
than in the lacy shadows on your grass.

You are the meeting place between
what's left for us, heaviness, nourishment,
and the passing touch
of infinite tenderness.

The water in the fountain at your center
is so confused by the marriage
of this paradox, it barely speaks of it,
drowsing in its ancient circle.

III

Jamais la terre n'est plus réelle
que dans tes branches, ô verger blond,
ni plus flottante que dans la dentelle
que font tes ombres sur le gazon.

Là se rencontre ce qui nous reste,
ce qui pèse et ce qui nourrit
avec le passage manifeste
de la tendresse infinie.

Mais à ton centre, la calme fontaine,
presque dormant en son ancien rond,
de ce contraste parle à peine,
tant en elle il se confond.

IV

What becomes of the grace
of all those irrelevant gods,
obliged by their rough beginnings
to behave like good little children?

They make fruit round
(a divine occupation), they play
hide-and-seek behind a curtain
of noise from hungry insects.

They never disappear
no matter how often they're abandoned;
the ones who sometimes threaten us
are the gods with idle hands.

IV

De leur grâce, que font-ils,
tous ces dieux hors d'usage,
qu'un passé rustique engage
à être sages et puérils?

Comme voilés par le bruit
des insectes qui butinent,
ils arrondissent les fruits
(occupation divine).

Car aucun jamais ne s'efface,
tant soit-il abandonné;
ceux qui parfois nous menacent
sont des dieux inoccupés.

V

What memories are evoked, what hopes, dear orchard,
    when I look around at you?
You are a flock of abundance; your shepherd meditates
    as you graze.

Let me look through your branches, contemplate
    the day turning toward night.
It's Sunday: you worked and I rested,
    but did resting do me any good?

What could be more right than being this shepherd?
    Is it possible that today I left
a trace of my peace on your apples?
    Because, as you know, I am leaving . . . .

V

Ai-je des souvenirs, ai-je des espérances,
    en te regardant, mon verger?
Tu te repais autour de moi, ô troupeau d'abondance,
    et tu fais penser ton berger.

Laisse-moi contempler au travers de tes branches
    la nuit qui va commencer.
Tu as travaillé; pour moi c'était un dimanche—
    mon repos, m'a-t-il avancé?

D'être berger, qu'y a-t-il de plus juste en somme?
    Se peut-il qu'un peu de ma paix
aujourd'hui soit entrée doucement dans tes pommes?
    Car tu sais bien, je m'en vais . . . .

VI

Wasn't this whole orchard
the bright dress around your shoulders?
And didn't you feel the comfort
of sinking your feet into its grass?

How often it refused to boast,
impressed us instead by expanding;
it was the orchard and the waning hour
that broke through your reluctance.

Sometimes you had a book. But your gaze,
haunted by many distractions,
followed the slow play of patterns
changing in the mirror of shadows.

VI

N'était-il pas, ce verger, tout entier,
ta robe claire, autour de tes épaules?
Et n'as-tu pas senti combien console
son doux gazon qui pliait sous ton pied?

Que de fois, au lieu de promenade,
il s'imposait en devenant tout grand;
et c'était lui et l'heure qui s'évade
qui passaient par ton être hésitant.

Un livre parfois t'accompagnait . . . .
Mais ton regard, hanté de concurrences,
au miroir de l'ombre poursuivait
un jeu changeant de lentes ressemblances.

VII

Glad orchard, expanding, perfecting
the countless designs of all these fruits,
confident that your ancient instincts
will bow to the urgency of youth,

what beautiful work, what order is yours!
It expresses itself in your twisted limbs
that then, charmed by power,
burst into the quiet air.

Your dangers and mine, aren't they brothers,
O orchard, O my brother?
Approaching us is the same far-off wind
that makes us both austere and tender.

VII

Heureux verger, tout tendu à parfaire
de tous ses fruits les innombrables plans,
et qui sait bien son instinct séculaire
plier à la jeunesse d'un instant.

Quel beau travail, quel ordre que le tien!
Qui tant insiste dans les branches torses,
mais qui enfin, enchanté de leur force,
déborde dans un calme aérien.

Tes dangers et les miens, ne sont-ils point
tout fraternels, ô verger, ô mon frère?
Un même vent, nous venant de loin,
nous force d'être tendres et austères.

All the Joys of the Ancestors

All the joys of the ancestors
flow through us and build,
their hearts, high with hunting,
their silent repose

by a dying fire . . .
and when life deserts us
in moments of drought,
we still have them, who fill us.

How many women took refuge here
to keep from falling apart,
the way an intermission provides respite
during a mediocre play.

Dressed in sorrow no one
wants to wear these days,
they look stronger leaning
on the blood of the old ones.

And the children, the children!
Those whom fate frowns upon
find in us a pretext
to keep on living.

30

Toutes les joies des aïeux
ont passé en nous et s'amassent;
leur cœur, ivre de chasse,
leur repos silencieux

devant un feu presque éteint . . . .
Si dans les instants arides
de nous notre vie se vide,
d'eux nous restons tout pleins.

Et combien de femmes ont du
en nous se sauver, intactes,
comme dans l'entr'acte
d'une pièce qui n'a pas plu—

parées d'un malheur qu'aujourd'hui
personne ne veut ni ne porte,
elles paraissent fortes
appuyées sur le sang d'autrui.

Et des enfants, des enfants!
Tous ceux que le sort refuse,
en nous exercent la ruse
d'exister pourtant.

Interior Portrait

It's not memories of you
that hold you within me,
nor the sheer
force of longing.

It's the way any slow
tender gesture
takes my very blood
on an ardent detour.

I have no need
to see you appear.
Being born was enough
to lose you a little less.

31: Portrait Intérieur

Ce ne sont pas des souvenirs
qui, en moi, t'entretiennent;
tu n'es pas non plus mienne
par la force d'un beau désir.

Ce qui te rend présente,
c'est le détour ardent
qu'une tendresse lente
décrit dans mon propre sang.

Je suis sans besoin
de te voir apparaître;
Il m'a suffi de naître
pour te perdre un peu moins.

This Hand

How will I recognize
the sweet life that was?
Perhaps by studying
the imagery in the lines

and wrinkles of my palm,
formed by closing
this hand of nothing
around the void.

32

Comment encore reconnaître
ce que fut la douce vie?
En contemplant peut-être
dans ma paume l'imagerie

de ces lignes et de ces rides
que l'on entretient
en fermant sur le vide
cette main de rien.

Elegy

How many ports, I ask you, and in them
how many doors might open to you,
through how many windows
can we see your life and your work.

How many winged seeds of the future
did the storm bring, according to its whim
one balmy holiday,
that will come to flower because of you.

How many lives will continue to echo,
and given the altitude at which you flew
while in this world,
a great void is no longer so hollow.

34

Combien de ports pourtant, et dans ces ports
combien de portes, t'accueillant peut-être,
combien de fenêtres
d'où l'on voit ta vie et ton effort.

Combien de grains ailés de l'avenir
qui, transportés au gré de la tempête,
un tendre jour de fête
verront leur floraison t'appartenir.

Combien de vies qui toujours se répondent;
et par l'essor que prend ta propre vie
en étant de ce monde,
quel gros néant à jamais compromis.

A Parting Melody

Since everything passes,
let's sing a parting melody,
a song of our own making
that will quench our grief.

Let's use love and art
to praise our losses,
and let's do it more quickly
than what departs.

36

Puisque tout passe, faisons
la mélodie passagère;
celle qui nous désaltère
aura de nous raison.

Chantons ce qui nous quitte
avec amour et art;
soyons plus vite
que le rapide départ.

The Soul-Bird

Often we plod
through thick fog,
while the soul-bird takes off
before us, balances

on a gentle sky.
This is how
our grief learns
the art of falling.

37

Souvent au-devant de nous
l'âme-oiseau s'élance;
c'est un ciel plus doux
qui déjà la balance,

pendant que nous marchons
sous des nuées épaisses.
Tout en peinant, profitons
de son ardente adresse.

Angel-Eye View

Seen by Angels, the crowns of trees
are roots that drink the skies,
and deep underground, the roots of the beech
seem to them like silent peaks.

Do they see a transparent earth
opposite a body-solid sky?
This ardent earth, where every wellspring
laments the forgotten dead.

38

Vues des Anges, les cimes des arbres peut-être
sont des racines, buvant les cieux;
et dans le sol, les profondes racines d'un hêtre
leur semblent des faîtes silencieux.

Pour eux, la terre, n'est-elle point transparente
en face d'un ciel, plein comme un corps?
Cette terre ardente, où se lamente
auprès des sources l'oubli des morts.

Friends and Strangers

My friends, I honor each of you,
and this incomprehensible fleeting life
opened little by little
with every shy and gentle glance.

How many times do we bring someone into being
instead of halting his disappearance,
when we take the trouble to hold him
in a look or a gesture.

Strangers. They play a leading role
in the fate of each passing day.
So take good aim at my worried heart,
stranger, when you lift your gaze.

39

Ô mes amis, vous tous, je ne renie
aucun de vous; ni même ce passant
qui n'était de l'inconcevable vie
qu'un doux regard ouvert et hésitant.

Combien de fois un être, malgré lui,
arrête de son œil ou de son geste
l'imperceptible fuite d'autrui,
en lui rendant un instant manifeste.

Les inconnus. Ils ont leur large part
à notre sort que chaque jour complète.
Précise bien, ô inconnue discrète,
mon cœur distrait, en levant ton regard.

Seeing Double

A swan moves on the water,
surrounding itself entirely,
a gliding tableau,
like the moments
when the one we love
is all space in motion.

She approaches, doubled
like the swan, floating
on the soul's uneasy pond
that superimposes upon her
a wavy image
of happiness and doubt.

40

Un cygne avance sur l'eau
tout entouré de lui-même,
comme un glissant tableau;
ainsi à certains instants
un être que l'on aime
est tout un espace mouvant.

Il se rapproche, doublé,
comme ce cygne qui nage,
sur notre âme troublée . . .
qui à cet être ajoute
la tremblante image
de bonheur et de doute.

Life Expressing Variety

Take the horse drinking at the fountain,
take a falling leaf that grazes our shoulder,
a cupped hand, a mouth bursting
with news it doesn't dare tell—

such is life expressing variety,
such are the sleepwalking dreams of pain.
Would someone with a peaceful heart
please search humanity and console it?

43
Tel cheval qui boit à la fontaine,
telle feuille qui en tombant nous touche,
telle main vide, ou telle bouche
qui nous voudrait parler et qui ose à peine—

autant de variations de la vie qui s'apaise,
autant de rêves de la douleur qui somnole:
ô que celui dont le cœur est à l'aise
cherche la créature et la console.

Spring

I

Notes of rising sap
that swell in the instrument
of all these trees,
accompany our song,
all too brief!

Nature, your abundance
resounds in the intricate
arpeggios of your abandon.
We hum along
for a few short measures,

and when we are silenced
others will carry on . . .
but for now, how can I
offer you this heart
large with yielding?

44: Printemps

I

Ô mélodie de la sève
qui dans les instruments
de tous ces arbres s'élève—
accompagne le chant
de notre voix trop brève.

C'est pendant quelques mesures
seulement que nous suivons
les multiples figures
de ton long abandon,
ô abondante nature.

Quand il faudra nous taire,
d'autres continueront . . .
mais à présent comment faire
pour te rendre mon
grand cœur complémentaire?

II

The arrival of joy
is eagerly awaited:
earth and everything in it
will soon delight us.

From our front row seat
we can see and hear,
and protect ourselves
when it becomes too much.

We think it's not personal,
but from where we sit
this emotional drama hits a bit
too close to home.

II

Tout se prépare et va
vers la joie manifeste;
la terre et tout le reste
bientôt nous charmera.

Nous serons bien placés
pour tout voir, tout entendre;
on devra même se défendre
et parfois dire: assez!

Encor si on était dedans;
mais l'excellente place
est un peu trop en face
de ce jeu émouvant.

III

Suddenly, for the old, lifeblood
mounting into capillaries means
a year too steep to climb, a year
that prepares them for departure.

Nature thrusts forward.
It boils in arteries
intolerant of sharp demands,
it lashes out against bodies

that refuse such wild adventure,
that harden instead, to survive.
So the earth, enduring and indifferent,
easily wins the game.

III

Montée des sèves dans les capillaires
qui tout à coup démontre aux vieillards
l'année trop raide qu'ils ne monteront guère
et qui en eux prépare le départ.

Leur corps (tout offensé par cet élan
de la nature brute qui ignore
que ces artères où elle bout encore
supportent mal un ordre impatient)

refuse la trop brusque aventure;
et pendant qu'il se raidit, méfiant,
pour subsister à sa façon, il rend
le jeu facile à la terre dure.

IV

It's the sap that kills,
that sudden air of insolence
floating through the streets,
taking the old and the hesitant.

All who lack the strength
to beat their own wings
are invited to the divorce
that will marry them with the earth.

It's sweetness that stabs them
with its sharpened point,
and those who still resist
are done in by a caress.

IV

C'est la sève qui tue
les vieux et ceux qui hésitent,
lorsque cet air insolite
flotte soudain dans les rues.

Tous ceux qui n'ont plus la force
de se sentir des ailes,
sont invités au divorce
qui à la terre les mêle.

C'est la douceur qui les perce
de sa pointe suprême,
et la caresse renverse
ceux qui résistent quand même.

V

What would the priceless
sensation of sweetness
be worth if it didn't
inspire fear?

It is so far beyond
every violence
that when it pounces,
we are defenseless.

V

Que vaudrait la douceur
si elle n'était capable,
tendre et ineffable,
de nous faire peur?

Elle surpasse tellement
toute la violence
que, lorsqu'elle s'élance,
nul ne se défend.

VI

In winter, death the murderer
enters all the houses
looking for sister and father,
playing his violin.

But when the earth stirs
under the spade of spring,
death runs through the streets,
greeting passers-by.

VI

En hiver, la mort meurtrière
entre dans les maisons;
elle cherche la sœur, le père,
et leur joue du violon.

Mais quand la terre remue
sous la bêche du printemps,
la mort court dans les rues
et salue les passants.

VII

It was from Adam's side
that Eve was pulled,
but where does she go to die
when her life is full?

Will Adam be her tomb?
Is there no other way for her
than to find her ultimate home
closed up inside a man?

VII

C'est de la côté d'Adam
qu'on a retiré Ève;
mais quand sa vie s'achève,
où va-t-elle, mourant?

Adam serait-il son tombeau?
Faut-il, lorsqu'elle se lasse,
lui ménager une place
dans un homme bien clos?

Light

Can it be this light
that gives us the world?
Or is it the shadow, new
and tender as it trembles,
that keeps us here?
That shadow resembles us,
trembles and twists
around whatever holds it up.
The shadows of frail foliage
that fall on path and field
make a sudden movement
that announces their kinship to us,
the way we are blended
with the young, clear light.

45

Cette lumière peut-elle
tout un monde nous rendre?
Est-ce plutôt la nouvelle
ombre, tremblante et tendre,
qui nous rattache à lui?
Elle qui tant nous ressemble
et qui tourne et tremble
autour d'un étrange appui.
Ombres des feuilles frêles,
sur le chemin et le pré,
geste soudain familier
qui nous adopte et nous mêle
à la trop neuve clarté.

Winter's United Silence

Winter's united silence
is replaced in the air
by the silence of warbling:
each voice rushing in
contributes a brushstroke
to perfect the image.

But the heart lives
far beyond
the whole complex
design of this silence, full
of unspeakable audacity,
only a starting point.

47

Le silence uni de l'hiver
est remplacé dans l'air
par un silence à ramage;
chaque voix qui accourt
y ajoute un contour,
y parfait une image.

Et tout cela n'est que le fond
de ce qui serait l'action
de notre cœur qui surpasse
le multiple dessin
de ce silence plein
d'inexprimable audace.

Nature Reveals Herself

There is a sublime moment,
between the misty mask and the verdant one,
when nature reveals herself
more fully than is her custom.

What beauty! Look at her shoulder,
the courage to be that transparent. . . .
Soon she'll play her role again
in summer's grassy theater.

48

Entre le masque de brume
et celui de verdure,
voici le moment sublime où la nature
se montre davantage que de coutume.

Ah, la belle! Regardez son épaule
et cette claire franchise qui ose . . . .
Bientôt de nouveau elle jouera un rôle
dans la pièce touffue que l'été compose.

The Flame

Out is the candle, and space
reclaims the room; we feel
the fire graze our cheeks,
a homeless, suffering flame.

Let's bury it in the subtle grave
behind our eyelids,
and cry like a mother who knows
all about danger.

51

À la bougie éteinte,
dans la chambre rendue à l'espace,
on est frôlé par la plainte
de feu la flamme sans place.

Faisons-lui un subtil
tombeau sous notre paupière,
et pleurons comme une mère
son très familier péril.

The Approach

The long life of the landscape, the bell,
the pure deliverance of evening—
all this prepares us for the approach
of a kindly, unfamiliar figure. . . .

Our life goes on, strangely suspended
between the faraway bow and the stab of the arrow,
between a world that hesitates to seize the angel
and She whose powerful presence prevents it.

52

C'est le paysage longtemps, c'est une cloche,
c'est du soir la délivrance si pure—;
mais tout cela en nous prépare l'approche
d'une nouvelle, d'une tendre figure . . . .

Ainsi nous vivons dans un embarras très étrange
entre l'arc lointain et la trop pénétrante flèche:
entre le monde trop vague pour saisir l'ange
et Celle qui, par trop de présence, l'empêche.

A Question

We arrange and rearrange
these words every which way,
but will this ever result
in anything worthy of the rose?

If we tolerate the strange
pretense of this game, it's only
to provide sport for the angel,
who comes to tease us a bit.

53

On arrange et on compose
les mots de tant de façons,
mais comment arriverait-on
à égaler une rose?

Si on supporte l'étrange
prétention de ce jeu,
c'est que, parfois, un ange
le dérange un peu.

In the Eyes of Animals

In the eyes of animals I've seen
lasting peace, the impartial
calm of nature
that cannot be shaken.

Every animal knows what fear is;
nevertheless, it moves along,
and on its field of plenty
grazes a presence
that has no taste for elsewhere.

54

J'ai vu dans l'œil animal
la vie paisible qui dure,
le calme impartial
de l'imperturbable nature.

La bête connaît la peur;
mais aussitôt elle avance
et sur son champ d'abondance
broute une présence
qui n'a pas le goût d'ailleurs.

The Doe

Doe, the deep, ancient beauty
of forests flows in your eyes,
circles of trust shot through
with utter fear.

The lively grace of your leaping
expresses all these things,
yet nothing can shake
a look of calm unknowing
on your face.

57: La Biche

Ô la biche: quel bel intérieur
d'anciennes forêts dans tes yeux abonde;
combien de confiance ronde
mêlée à combien de peur.

Tout cela, porté par la vive
gracilité de tes bonds.
Mais jamais rien n'arrive
à cette impossessive
ignorance de ton front.

Let's Chat for a While

Let's stay here and chat for a while.
I'm the one who stopped again tonight,
and again you're the one who's listening.

Later others will play at being
neighbors on this road under trees
whose lovely shade we're borrowing.

58

Arrêtons-nous un peu, causons.
C'est encore moi, ce soir, qui m'arrête,
c'est encore vous qui m'écoutez.

Un peu plus tard d'autres joueront
aux voisins sur la route
sous ces beaux arbres que l'on se prête.